MALCOLM X

GARLAND REFERENCE LIBRARY
OF SOCIAL SCIENCE
(VOL. 288)

(MALCOLM X)
A Comprehensive Annotated Bibliography

Timothy V. Johnson

GARLAND PUBLISHING, INC. · NEW YORK & LONDON
1986

Library of Congress Cataloging-in-Publication Data
Johnson, Timothy V., 1952–
Malcolm X : a comprehensive annotated bibliography.

(Garland reference library of social science ;
vol. 288)
Includes indexes.
1. X, Malcolm, 1925–1965—Bibliography.　I. Title.
II. Series: Garland reference library of social science ;
v. 288.
Z8989.7.J64　1986　　016.297'87'0924　　84-48401
[BP223.28.L57]
ISBN 0-8240-8790-9 (alk. paper)

Printed on acid-free, 250-year-life paper
Manufactured in the United States of America

CONTENTS

INTRODUCTION

Few other figures in U.S. history have captured the imagination of the Afro-American community, the white community, or the press, as Malcolm X did during and after his lifetime. The very fact that his _Autobiography_ is still on the reading list of many freshman composition classes is reflective of this.

In addition, Malcolm X is still a very popular subject for term papers. While I was a Northwestern University as the African-American Studies Bibliographer, I consistently received requests for information on Malcolm X. Unfortunately, at that time there was no adequate bibliography available. In order to fill this need, I began to compile this bibliography in 1980.

In 1984 Greenwood Press published a selected bibliography on Malcolm X. After looking at their bibliography I decided to continue working on mine. Although the Greenwood book is very useful there are some serious drawbacks to it. Most importantly the lack of a subject index renders it difficult to use. Secondly, the absence of citations from African newspapers leaves an important gap in the writings on Malcolm. Thirdly, the lack of annotations for Malcolm's own writings and speeches is problematic. And finally, the book is too cluttered with references to Malcolm that only consist of one or two pages. In spite of its handicaps, I did find it useful for several citations that I would have missed.

This bibliography is meant to be comprehensive in its coverage of books, articles, and taped speeches. The news articles give comprehensive coverage from Malcolm's rise to prominence until his assassination and the ensuing trial. I have attempted to cover news articles written after the trial that concern the subsequent revelations in the FBI documents uncovered through the Freedom of Information Act.

The first section consists of writings and speeches by Malcolm. They are categorized by the type of material, i.e., books, articles, taped speeches, etc., with each speech being annotated.

The second section consists of books and dissertations written about Malcolm. These were collected by searching through the traditional bibliographic tools.

The third section is articles. Most of these are scholarly journal articles and articles from popular magazines. They are arranged alphabetically by author.

The fourth section is news articles. These news articles are divided into four different categories. Firstly, there are reports from the mainstream press. These are largely made up of articles from the New York Times, the newspaper with the most consistent coverage of Malcolm. Secondly, there are reports from the Afro-American press. These are mostly from the Amsterdam News, a Harlem-based paper that covered Malcolm from the late 1950s until his death. Third, there is the left-wing press. Most of these citations were gathered from a manual checking of the Militant, the newspaper of the Socialist Workers Party. The Militant probably provided the best, and least biased coverage of Malcolm, often reprinting the entire text of his speeches. Fourth, there is a section on articles from the African press.

All of the citations in section four are arranged chronologically with each article annotated. In addition each citation includes a reference to the word length of each article.

Section five is a listing of the FBI files on Malcolm X that were published by Scholarly Resources. Because they are arranged on the microfilm by the date they were received, they follow no logical order. For this section I have listed them in the sequence in which they are listed on the microfilm. I have added the date of each report in order to ease access to the files.

Section six is book reviews of all the books listed in sections one and two. They are listed alphabetically by the title of the book.

The last sections are author and subject indexes.

In any endeavor such as this there are a number of people and institutions to thank. I would like to thank Northwestern University's Special Collection and News-Microtext Departments, and the Schomberg Library of the New York Public Library for the use of their collections. I

would also like to thank the University of Illinois-Chicago
Library for an FDAC grant that allowed me to travel to New
York to use the Schomberg Library. Last, but certainly not
least, I would like to thank Maggie Newman for typing the
manuscript and providing editorial assistance.

July 5, 1985
Chicago, Illinois

Malcolm X

I WORKS BY MALCOLM X

Books

1-1 Autobiography of Malcolm X. New York: Grove Press,
     1965.

       This work, written with the assistance of Alex
     Haley, covers Malcolm's early life through his break
     with the Nation of Islam and his trip to Mecca. In the
     afterword Haley details the circumstances around the
     writing of the book and updates it to Malcolm's
     assassination.

1-2 By Any Means Necessary. New York: Pathfinder Press,
     1970.

       This collection of material by Malcolm is meant to
     be a companion volume to Malcolm X Speaks. It includes
     the following pieces:

       1. "An Interview by A. B. Spellman."
          This interview was held just after Malcolm left the
          Nation of Islam. In the interview he insists that
          he is still a follower of Elijah Muhammad. He com-
          ments on the split and his intention to carry out
          the Muslim program outside of the Nation of Islam,
          and gives his views on working with existing civil
          rights organizations.

       2. "Answers to Questions at the Militant Labor Forum."
          The question and answer period following the
          speech, "The Black Revolution" (citation #1-5(4)).
          Malcolm fields questions on Karl Marx, the Freedom
          Now Party, integration, and self-defense.

       3. "The Founding Rally of the OAAU."
          Malcolm outlines the Constitution of the OAAU. In

the section after the Constitution he discusses the
relation of white supporters to the OAAU and
announces a program of political education, aimed
at registering voters in Harlem.

4. "Harlem and the Political Machines."
   An excerpt from a radio broadcast recorded in July
   1964. In the discussion Malcolm addresses voter
   registration and Adam Clayton Powell.

5. "The Second Rally of the OAAU."
   In this speech, delivered in July 1964, Malcolm
   discusses independent politics in the Afro-American
   community. In the question and answer period he
   discusses the relation of whites to the civil
   rights movement and the relation of Afro-Americans
   to Africa.

6. "A Letter from Cairo."
   In this letter, written in August 1964, Malcolm
   discusses his concept of internationalizing the
   Afro-American struggle and remarks on some of the
   internal problems within the OAAU.

7. "At a Meeting in Paris."
   This is a question and answer period held after a
   speech Malcolm delivered in Paris in November 1964
   (see citation #1-15 for speech). Malcolm discusses
   nonviolence and integration.

8. "An Exchange on Casualties in the Congo."
   Excerpt from a radio show taped in August 1964. In
   the exchange printed here Malcolm debates with a
   professor over the number of Africans killed in the
   Congo during the period of colonialism.

9. "The Homecoming Rally of the OAAU."
   In this speech, delivered upon Malcolm's return
   from Africa, he discusses some of his experiences
   in Africa and speaks of the importance of estab-
   lishing a connection between Afro-Americans and
   Africans.

10. "The Young Socialist Interview."
    In this interview, taped in January 1965, Malcolm
    discusses his break with the Nation of Islam, black
    nationalism, and his trips to Africa.

11. "On Being Barred from France."
    Transcript of a telephone conversation between
    Malcolm and a supporter of his in France, recorded
    after Malcolm was denied entry into France.
    Malcolm speculates on his being denied entry and
    discusses racism and the civil rights movement.

12. "Short Statements."
    A selection of statements on a variety of subjects
    including the role of women, socialism, and youth.

1-3   The End of White World Supremacy. New York: Merlin
      House, 1971.

      This is a selection of four speeches by Malcolm,
all given while he was a minister in the Nation of
Islam. The editor, Benjamin Karim, was a close assoc-
iate of Malcolm's. In the introduction Karim details
some personal recollections of Malcolm.

1. "Black Man's History."
   Malcolm relates the history of Afro-Americans,
   using Biblical parallels and Nation of Islam
   eschatology.

2. "The Black Revolution."
   Given at a forum at the Abyssinian Baptist Church
   in Harlem, Malcolm discusses the Nation of Islam
   position on separation. Includes a short question
   and answer period.

3. "The Old Negro and the New Negro."
   In this speech-interview Malcolm comments on the
   Muslim image in the white press, the civil rights
   movement, and Dr. Martin Luther King.

4. "God's Judgment of White America (The Chickens Are
   Coming Home to Roost)."
   In this speech, the last Malcolm made as a minister
   in the Nation of Islam, Malcolm discusses biblical
   prophecy about the end of the world and gives his
   views on the March on Washington.

1-4   Malcolm X on Afro-American History. New York: Inter-
      national Socialist Review, 1967.

In this speech Malcolm discusses ancient history, Afro-American history, and American slavery. Includes a question and answer period in which he discusses the role black nationalists can play in the civil rights movement.

1-5   Malcolm X Speaks. New York: Merit, 1967.

This collection is the first major compilation of Malcolm's speeches.

  1. "Message to the Grassroots."
     One of the last speeches by Malcolm as a Nation of Islam minister. In it he discusses the nature of revolutions and criticizes the March on Washington.

  2. "A Declaration of Independence."
     Text of the press conference where Malcolm officially broke with the Nation of Islam and announced the formation of the Muslim Mosque, Inc. He still professes his belief in the program and philosophy of the Nation of Islam.

  3. "Ballot or the Bullet."
     In his first major speech after the split, Malcolm discusses the possibilities of using the electoral arena to address grievances. He also discusses the philosophy of black nationalism as interpreted by the Muslim Mosque, Inc. The version of this speech printed here is the one delivered in Cleveland.

  4. "The Black Revolution."
     Given at a meeting of the Militant Labor Forum; Malcolm discusses the use of the ballot to effect a "bloodless" revolution.

  5. "Letters from Abroad."
     In these letters, written during Malcolm's 1964 trip to Africa, he begins to reevaluate his racial positions and puts forward the concept of Pan-Africanism.

  6. "The Harlem 'Hate Gang' Scare."
     In this symposium at the Militant Labor Forum, Malcolm discusses terrorism and police brutality. In a question and answer period he addresses socialism, integration, and religion.

7. "Appeal to African Heads of State."
   Text of a memorandum Malcolm circulated at the
   meeting of the OAU. In it he explains his concept
   of "internationalizing" the Afro-American struggle
   and making it a case of human rights, not civil
   rights. He requests the help of the African heads
   of state to bring the Afro-American question before
   the U.N. Printed with the memorandum in this book
   is an interview with Malcolm where he discusses the
   OAU meeting.

8. "At the Audubon."
   Speech at an OAAU rally. Malcolm discusses Castro
   and Cuba, and the U.S. interference in the Congo.

9. "With Mrs. Fannie Lou Hamer."
   Speech given at a rally in support of the Mississippi Freedom Democratic Party. Malcolm discusses
   politics in the South and the Southern influence in
   the Democratic Party.

10. "At the Audubon."
    Speech at an OAAU rally. Malcolm discusses current
    political situations in Egypt and the Congo.

11. "To Mississippi Youth."
    Speech to a SNCC-sponsored delegation of youth from
    Mississippi. Malcolm discusses his views on the
    civil rights movement and nonviolence.

12. "Prospects for Freedom in 1965."
    Delivered at the Militant Labor Forum. Malcolm
    discusses his trip to Africa, the civil rights
    movement, and the OAAU.

13. "After the Bombing."
    Speech given in Detroit one week before Malcolm's
    assassination and one day after his house had been
    firebombed. Malcolm discusses Pan-Africanism and
    President Kennedy's relationship to the civil
    rights movement.

14. "Confrontation with an Expert."
    Excerpt from a radio interview program where
    Malcolm debates with a sociologist. The topic of
    the confrontation is extremism, Malcolm, and the
    Nation of Islam.

15. "Last Answers and Interviews."
A selection of questions and answers on a variety
of topics, including racism, intermarriage, black
nationalism, and a return to Africa.

1-6 Malcolm X Talks to Young People. New York: Pathfinder,
1967.

A compilation of citations #1-2(10) and #1-5(11).

1-7 Speeches of Malcolm X at Harvard. New York: Morrow,
1968.

This is a collection of three speeches edited by
Harvard professor Archie Epps.

1. "The Harvard Law School Forum of March 24, 1961."
In this speech, given while Malcolm was still a
Muslim minister, he espouses the Nation of Islam
proposal for separation.

2. "The Leverett House Forum of March 18, 1964."
Malcolm discusses black nationalism and the civil
rights movement.

3. "The Harvard Law School Forum of December 16,
1964."
Malcolm discusses events in the Congo and the civil
rights movement. Includes a question and answer
period where Malcolm addresses the concept "Afro-
American" and Dr. King's winning the Nobel Prize.

1-8 Two Speeches by Malcolm X. New York: Pioneer Press,
1965.

Includes citations #1-4(2), #1-5(4), and excerpts
from #1-2(10).

Articles

1-9 "Afro-American History." International Socialist
Review 28:3 Mar-Apr 1967.

Same as citation #1-4.

1-10   "Ballot or the Bullet." In The Negro Speaks, ed. Jamye
       and McDonald Williams. New York: Noble and Noble,
       1970, p. 245.

       Same as citation #1-5(3).

1-11   "Ballot or the Bullet." In A Choice of Words, ed.
       James Andrews. New York: Harper & Row, 1973, p.
       135.

       Same as citation #1-5(3).

1-12   "Ballot or the Bullet." In Voice of Black America, ed.
       Phillip Foner. New York: Simon and Schuster, 1972,
       p. 985.

       Same as citation #1-5(3).

1-13   "Ballot or the Bullet." In Relevant Rhetoric, ed.
       Irving Rein. New York: Free Press, 1969.

       Same as citation #1-5(3).

1-14   "Black Revolution as Part of World-Wide Struggle."
       Militant, 27 Apr 1964, p. 4.

       Same as citation #1-5(4).

1-15   "Black Struggle in the United States." Presence
       Africaine 26:8, 1965.

       A short statement by Malcolm at a meeting in Paris.
       He discusses the relationship of Africa to Afro-
       Americans and mentions his attempt to bring the Afro-
       American question before the U.N. The question and
       answer period following the statement is the same as
       citation #1-2(7).

1-16   "Communication and Reality." In Malcolm X: The Man and
       His Times, ed. John Henrik Clarke. New York:
       Macmillan, 1969, p. 307.

In this speech before domestic Peace Corps workers, Malcolm restates his position on self-defense, racism, and the relation between Africa and Afro-Americans.

1-17   "Definition of a Revolution." In <u>Malcolm X: The Man</u> <u>and His Times</u>, ed. John Henrik Clarke. New York: Macmillan, 1969, p. 273.

An excerpt from "Message to the Grassroots" (citation #1-5(1)).

1-18   "God's Angry Men." <u>Amsterdam News</u>.

A series of columns written by Malcolm covering the basic beliefs of the Nation of Islam. Columns are individually annotated in Section 4B under the following citations: #4B-4, #4B-6, #4B-9, #4B-10, #4B-11, and #4B-12.

1-19   "God's Judgment of White America." In <u>Malcolm X: The</u> <u>Man and His Times</u>, ed. John Henrik Clarke. New York: Macmillan, 1969, p. 282.

An excerpt from citation #1-3(4).

1-20   "God's Judgment of White America." <u>Evergreen Review</u> 5:54, Dec 1967.

Same as citation #1-3(4).

1-21   "James Farmer and Malcolm X: Debate on the Solution to America's Race Problem." In <u>Speeches by Black</u> <u>Americans</u>, ed. Daniel O'Neill. Encino, CA: Dickenson, 1971.

Text of a debate on separation versus integration. Malcolm, at that time still a Nation of Islam minister, insists that Afro-Americans want freedom, not integration. He argues for a separate state.

1-22   "James Farmer and Malcolm X: Debate on the Solution to America's Race Problem." <u>Dialogue Mazagine</u> 2:14, May 1962.

Same as citation #1-21.

1-23   "James Farmer and Malcolm X: Debate on the Solution to
           America's Race Problem." In Rhetoric of the Civil
           Rights Movement, ed. Haig Bosmagian. New York:
           Random House, 1969.

       Same as citation #1-21.

1-24   "Letter from Ghana." Amsterdam News, 28 Mar 1965, p.
           11.

       Text of a letter from Malcolm to the Amsterdam News
       written in May 1964. In the letter Malcolm advocates
       Pan-Africanism as a solution to the Afro-Americans'
       problems.

1-25   "Letter to Jackie Robinson." Amsterdam News, 30 Nov
           1963, p. 1.

       In this open letter Malcolm accuses Robinson of
       attempting to please whites by attacking him.

1-26   "Letters from Mecca." In Black Power Revolt, ed. Floyd
           Barbour. Boston: Extending Horizons Books, 1968,
           p. 240.

       Excerpts from citation #1-5(5).

1-27   "Malcolm X Proclaims Muhammad as Man of the Hour." In
           Rhetoric of Racial Revolt, ed. Roy Hill. Denver:
           Golden Bell Press, 1964, p. 304.

       In this speech, delivered at Yale University in
       1960, Malcolm explains the Nation of Islam position on
       separation.

1-28   "Malcolm X Talks to Young People." In Voice of Black
           America, ed. Phillip Foner. New York: Simon and
           Schuster, 1972, p. 1004.

       Excerpts from citation #1-6.

1-29 "The Muhammads, What Are They?" Amsterdam News, 6 Apr
         1957, p. 4.

      Malcolm explains the basic beliefs of the Nation of
Islam, including their positions on integration,
baptism, and diet.

1-30 "Muslim's Teachings." New York Times Magazine, 25 Aug
         1963, p. 2.

      A letter to the editor from Malcolm correcting dis-
tortions in an article that appeared in the New York
Times.

1-31 "The Negro's Fight." Egyptian Gazette, 25 Aug 1964, p.
         4.

      A discussion of the current stage of the civil
rights movement.

1-32 "Power in Defense of Freedom Is Greater than Power in
         Behalf of Tyranny." Militant, 25 Ja 1965, p. 4.

      Same as citation #1-5(12).

1-33 "Racism: The Cancer That Is Destroying America." In
         Malcolm X: The Man and His Times, ed. John Henrik
         Clarke. New York: Macmillan, 1969, p. 302.

      Malcolm explains how his pilgrimage to Mecca
changed his racial views. He discusses the need to
build a united front of all Afro-American organizations
and explains his goal of bringing the Afro-American
question before the U.N.

1-34 "Racism: The Cancer That Is Destroying America."
         Egyptian Gazette, 25 Aug 1965, p. 3.

      Same as citation #1-33.

1-35 "Second African Summit Conference." In Malcolm X: The
         Man and His Times, ed. John Henrik Clarke. New
         York: Macmillan, 1969, p. 294.

Text of a press release by Malcolm at the OAU
meeting. He surveys the importance of the meeting and
comments on how well he was received by the African
heads of state.

1-36 "Some Reflections on Negro History Week and the Role of
      Black People in History." In Malcolm X: The Man
      and His Times, ed. John Henrik Clarke. New York:
      Macmillan, 1969, p. 321.

      Excerpts from citation #1-9.

1-37 "Speech to African Summit Conference-Cairo, Egypt." In
      Malcolm X: The Man and His Times, ed. John Henrik
      Clarke. New York: Macmillan, 1969, p. 205.

      Same as citation #1-5(7).

1-38 "Telephone Conversation." In Malcolm X: The Man and
      His Times, ed. John Henrik Clarke. New York:
      Macmillan, 1969, p. 205.

      Same as citation #1-2(11).

1-39 "Text of a Statement by Malcolm X." Militant, 23 Mar
      1964, p. 6.

      Same as citation #1-5(2).

1-40 "Visit from the FBI." In Malcolm X: The Man and His
      Times, ed. John Henrik Clarke. New York:
      Macmillan, 1969, p. 182.

      A transcript from a tape Malcolm made of an FBI
      visit while he was under suspension from the Nation of
      Islam. The agents question him about the suspension
      and on his position on self-defense.

1-41 "We Are All Blood Brothers." Liberator 4:4, July 1964.

      A short article describing his trip to Africa and
      the Middle East. Describes meetings with representa-

tives of the Cuban, Chinese, Ghanian, and Algerian
governments.

1-42   "Where Is the American Negro Headed?" In Malcolm X:
       The Man and His Times, ed. John Henrik Clarke. New
       York: Macmillan, 1969, p. 149.

       A panel discussion Malcolm participated in during
       1961. Malcolm argues for separation.

                          Interviews

1-43   "Black Muslims and Civil Rights." In Freedom Now!, ed.
       Alan Westin. New York: Basic Books, 1964, p. 52.

       Excerpt from citation #1-52.

1-44   "The Black Vigilante." In Voices from the Sixties, ed.
       Pierre Berton. Garden City, NY: Doubleday, 1967,
       p. 31.

       In this interview taped in January 1965, Malcolm
       discusses why he left the Nation of Islam, racial
       intermarriage, and self-defense.

1-45   "Interview with Malcolm X." Monthly Review 16:14, May
       1964.

       Same as citation #1-2(1).

1-46   "Interview with Malcolm X." Young Socialist, Mar-Apr
       1965, p. 2.

       Same as citation #1-2(10).

1-47   "Malcolm X." In The Negro Protest, ed. Kenneth Clark.
       Boston: Beacon Press, 1963, p. 15.

       Text of an interview, held in 1963, in which
       Malcolm discusses his early life, imprisonment, and
       explains the Nation of Islam position on self-defense
       and separation.

1-48   "Malcolm X Talks with Kenneth B. Clarke." In Malcolm
         X: The Man and His Times, ed. John Henrik Clarke.
         New York: Macmillan, 1969, p. 168.

         Same as citation #1-46.

1-49   "Malcolm X: The Complexity of a Man in the Jungle."
         Village Voice, 25 Feb 1965, p. 1.

         An interview with reporter Marlene Nadle. Malcolm
         discusses black nationalism and the relation of whites
         to the civil rights movement.

1-50   "Malcolm X: The Final Interview." Flamingo (Ghana), Ja
         1965, p.

         Not available for annotation.

1-51   "Now It's a Negro Drive for Segregation." U.S. News
         and World Report, 30 Mar 1964, p. 38.

         Malcolm explains his position on a black political
         party, integration, self-defense, and a separate black
         nation.

1-52   "Playboy Interview: Malcolm X." Playboy 10:53, May
         1963.

         In this interview, conducted by Alex Haley, Malcolm
         discusses the philosophy of the Nation of Islam,
         comments on separation, and the civil rights movement.

1-53   "Playboy Interview: Malcolm X." In Playboy Interviews.
         Chicago: Playboy Press, 1967, p. 30.

         Same as citation #1-52.

                        Recorded Material

1-54   "African Revolution and Its Impact on the American
         Negro." In the Schomberg Center Oral History Tape
         Collection.

Same as citation #1-5(4).

1-55   "African Revolution and Its Effect on the Afro-
       American." In the Schomberg Center Oral History
       Tape Collection.

       At a rally held on December 12, 1964, Malcolm
       discusses black nationalism and the civil rights
       movement. Excerpts appear in citation #1-5(8).

1-56   "Ballot or the Bullet." In the Schomberg Center Oral
       History Tape Collection.

       Same as citation #1-5(3).

1-57   "Ballot or the Bullet." In the Schomberg Center Oral
       History Tape Collection.

       This speech, given in Detroit, is essentially the
       same as citation #1-5(3).

1-58   "Ballots or Bullets." First Amendment Records (LP-FAR
       100).

       Same as citation #1-5(3).

1-59   "Black Revolution." In the Schomberg Center Oral
       History Tape Collection.

       Same as citation #1-5(4).

1-60   "Crisis of Racism." In the Schomberg Center Oral
       History Tape Collection.

       Tape of speech given in May 1962. Malcolm
       discusses separation and the Nation of Islam
       philosophy.

1-61   "Harlem Emergency Rally in Support of Seating Missis-
       sippi Freedom Democratic Party Representatives in
       Congress." In the Schomberg Center Oral History
       Tape Collection.

Same as citation #1-5(9).

1-62   "Harlem Hate Gang Scare." In the Schomberg Center Oral
       History Tape Collection.

       Same as citation #1-5(6).

1-63   "Interview with Malcolm X and Harry Ring of WBAI." In
       the Schomberg Center Oral History Tape Collection.

       Recorded on January 28, 1965. Malcolm discusses
       his break with the Nation of Islam and U.S. foreign
       policy.

1-64   "Interview with Malcolm X at the London School of
       Economics." In the Schomberg Center Oral History
       Tape Collection.

       Recorded in February 1965, Malcolm discusses U.S.
       foreign policy and black nationalism.

1-65   "Malcolm on Afro-American History." In the Schomberg
       Center Oral History Tape Collection.

       Same as citation #1-4.

1-66   "Malcolm X . . . At His Best." WIL-CAS (MX-201/2).

       Excerpts from various recorded speeches.

1-67   "Malcolm X Speaking." Ethnic Records (E-1265).

       Not available for annotation.

1-68   "Malcolm X Speaks Again." 20 Grand (LP-100).

       Not available for annotation.

1-69   "Malcolm X Talks to Young People." Douglass (SD 795).

Same as citation #1-6.

1-70 "Malcolm X: The Last Message." Discos Hablandos (LP
      1300-1301).

      Not available for annotation.

1-71 "Message from Malcolm X." Audiofidelity (PHX 348).

      Excerpts from various speeches.

1-72 "Message to the Grassroots." Afro-American B & R (AA-
      1264).

      Same as citation #1-5(1).

1-73 "Prospects for Freedom in 1965." In the Schomberg
      Center Oral History Tape Collection.

      Same as citation #1-5(12).

1-74 "Speech of Malcolm X at CCNY." In the Schomberg Center
      Oral History Tape Collection.

      In this speech, recorded in 1963, Malcolm discusses
      the philosophy of the Nation of Islam.

1-75 "Young Socialist Interview." In the Schomberg Center
      Oral History Tape Collection.

      Same as citation #1-2(10).

II BOOKS AND DISSERTATIONS

2-1   Baldwin, James. One Day When I Was Lost: A Screenplay
        Based on the "Autobiography of Malcolm X." New
        York: Dial, 1973.

        Screenplay covering Malcolm's early life as a
        hustler and criminal through his rise in the leader-
        ship of the Nation of Islam, his conflict with Elijah
        Muhammad, and finally through his political changes
        after he left the Nation of Islam.

2-2   Breitman, George (ed.), Assassination of Malcolm X.
        New York: Pathfinder Press, 1976.

        A collection of essays by Breitman, Herman Porter,
        and Baxter Smith. Many of the essays first appeared
        in the Militant. The authors survey Malcolm's last
        year, the assassination and the trial. Much attention
        is given to discrepancies in the trial, with the
        authors asserting that Malcolm was the victim of a
        government conspiracy.

2-3   Breitman, George. Last Year of Malcolm X: The
        Evolution of a Revolutionary. New York: Merit,
        1967.

        An analysis of the last year of Malcolm's life.
        The author attempts to demonstrate how Malcolm evolved
        from a narrow nationalist viewpoint to a revolutionary
        nationalist viewpoint. He uses excerpts from Malcolm's
        speeches and his own interaction with Malcolm to
        validate his points.

2-4   Breitman, George. Malcolm X: The Man and His Ideas.
        New York: Pathfinder Press, 1965.

This pamphlet is taken from a speech delivered by Breitman. In it he attempts to assess the significance of Malcolm's political ideas. He details Malcolm's attitudes on alliances with progressive whites and his attitudes towards the Trotskyite Socialist Workers Party.

2-5   Clarke, John. Malcolm X: The Man and His Times. New York: Macmillan, 1969.

A collection of essays, some reprinted from other sources and some original, on Malcolm's life and his influence. All of the essays in this book are individually annotated in Section 3 of this bibliography.

2-6   Davis, Lenwood. Malcolm X: A Selected Bibliography. Westport, CT: Greenwood Press, 1984.

A major bibliography covering the most imortant books, articles, and audio-visual material by and about Malcolm. Some entries are annotated.

2-7   Deck, Alice. I Am Because We Are: Four Versions of the Common Voice in African and Afro-American Autobiography. Ph.D. Dissertation: State University of New York at Binghamton, 1980.

A literary study of black autobiography in which the author attempts to show how society and the family act as referents in the lives of oppressed people. Malcolm's autobiography is one of the works used to prove this point.

2-8   Epps, Archie. The Speeches of Malcolm X at Harvard. New York: William Morrow, 1969.

In Epps's introductory essays to this volume he surveys Malcolm's life, discusses the influence of imagery on Malcolm's speech, and makes some comments on Malcolm's changing political perspective.

2-9   Essien-Udom, E. U. Black Nationalism. Chicago:
        University of Chicago Press, 1962.

        One of the classic studies on the Nation of Islam.
        The vast majority of the book concerns the organiza-
        tion, history, and eschatology of the Nation of Islam,
        although the role of Malcolm in the Nation of Islam is
        mentioned throughout the book.

2-10   Goldman, Peter. Death and Life of Malcolm X. New
        York: Harper, 1973. Revised edition, Urbana, Ill.:
        University of Illinois Press, 1979.

        This major biography of Malcolm makes extensive use
        of newspaper reports, the autobiography, and personal
        interviews. The author's emphasis is on the split
        between Malcolm and the Nation of Islam and the last
        year of Malcolm's life. There are also extensive
        sections on the assassination and the trial. These
        sections are updated in the revised edition.

2-11   Harper, Frederick. Maslow's Concept of Self-
        actualization Compared with Personality Character-
        istics of Selected Black American Protestors:
        Martin Luther King, Jr., Malcolm X and Frederick
        Douglass. Ph.D. Dissertation: Florida State
        University, 1970.

        The study views the personality characteristics
        associated with the concept "self-actualization" and
        relates them to Malcolm, King, and Douglass. The
        author finds that each of the men share the "self-
        actualization" characteristics.

2-12   Hodges, John. The Quest for Selfhood in the Autobio-
        graphies of W. E. B. DuBois, Richard Wright, and
        Malcolm X. Ph.D. Dissertation: University of
        Chicago, 1980.

        The author studies the autobiographies of these
        three leaders in order to discover their path towards
        self-realization.

2-13   Jamal, Hakim. From the Dead Level: Malcolm X and
          Me. New York: Random House, 1972.

          Autobiography of a man who claimed to be Malcolm's
          cousin by marriage. (Researchers have cast doubt on
          this claim.) The book details the early life of the
          author, including his acquaintance with Malcolm before
          either joined the Nation of Islam. He also details
          their subsequent relationship until Malcolm's death,
          at which point the author was residing in Los Angeles
          and still active in the Nation of Islam.

2-14   Kofsky, Frank. Black Nationalism and the Revolution
          in Music. New York: Pathfinder Press, 1970.

          An attempt to discuss the ramifications of
          political protest on music. The author discusses the
          influence of Malcolm and the Afro-American movement on
          the development of progressive jazz musicians,
          particularly John Coltrane.

2-15   Lincoln, C. Eric. Black Muslims in America. Boston:
          Beacon, 1961.

          A study of the Nation of Islam by a prominent Afro-
          American theologian. Although the focus of the book
          is on the history and eschatology of the Nation of
          Islam, there is a considerable amount of material on
          Malcolm.

2-16   Lincoln University, Vail Memorial Library. Malcolm X:
          A Selected Bibliography. Chester County, PA:
          Lincoln University, 1969.

          A short (six pages) bibliography covering the major
          books and articles on Malcolm.

2-17   Lomax, Louis. To Kill a Black Man. Los Angeles:
          Holloway House, 1968.

          A popularized study of the lives of Malcolm and
          Martin Luther King.

2-18   Lomax, Louis. When the Word Is Given. Cleveland:
        World Publishing, 1963.

        Popularized study of the Nation of Islam. Includes
        several speeches by Malcolm when he was a Muslim
        minister.

2-19   Luellen, David. Ministers and Martyrs: Malcolm X and
        Martin Luther King, Jr. Ph.D. Dissertation: Ball
        State University, 1972.

        The author compares and contrasts the styles and
        ideas of Malcolm and King. Includes brief biographies
        of each and separate assessments of their styles and
        ideas.

2-20   McCauley, Mary. Alex Haley, A Southern Griot: A
        Literary Biography. Ph.D. Dissertation: George
        Peabody College for Teachers, 1983.

        A biography of Alex Haley, author of Malcolm's
        autobiography. Includes a chapter on the writing of
        the autobiography and details Haley's relationship to
        Malcolm.

2-21   McGuire, Robert. Continuity in Black Political
        Protest: The Thought of Booker T. Washington, W. E.
        B. DuBois, Marcus Garvey, Malcolm X, Joseph Casely
        Hayford, Joseph B. Danquah, and Kwame Nkrumah.
        Ph.D. Dissertation, Columbia University, 1974.

        Compares and contrasts seven Afro-American and
        African leaders in several areas, including religious
        influences, views on world politics, and the relation
        between Afro-Americans and Africans.

2-22   Maglangbayou, Shawna. Garvey, Lumumba, and Malcolm:
        National-Separatists. Chicago: Third World Press,
        1972.

        The chapter on Malcolm in this book argues that he
        never became an integrationist but remained a
        separatist and continued to see white people as the
        enemy of Afro-Americans. Insists that Malcolm was

misled by Arabs into thinking that there was no racial problem in Islamic countries.

2-23   Moore, William. On Identity and Consciousness of El Hajj Malik El Shabazz (Malcolm X). Ph.D. Dissertation: University of California, Santa Cruz, 1974.

Not available for annotation.

2-24   Onwubu, Chukwuemeka. Black Ideologies and the Sociology of Knowledge: The Public Response to the Protest Thoughts and Teachings of Martin Luther King, Jr., and Malcolm X. Ph.D. Dissertation: Michigan State University, 1975.

The author surveys the Afro-American community of Albuquerque, New Mexico to analyze the public reaction to King and Malcolm. Particular attention is paid to the role of the media.

2-25   Paris, Peter. Black Leaders in Conflict: Joseph H. Jackson, Martin Luther King, Jr., Malcolm X, and Adam Clayton Powell, Jr. New York: Pilgrim Press, 1978.

The author attempts to demonstrate that there was an underlying unity in the thought of these four Afro-American leaders. His point is that although their political philosophies appear contradictory, there is actually a basis for united action among their respective followings.

2-26   Payne, James. A Content Analysis of Speeches and Written Documents of Six Black Spokesmen: Frederick Douglass, Booker T. Washington, Marcus Garvey, W. E. B. DuBois, Martin Luther King, Jr., and Malcolm X. Ph.D. Dissertation: Florida State University, 1973.

Using the tools of content analysis, the author examines the written and recorded speeches of these leaders, finding similarities on some aspects of their speech patterns.

2-27   Randall, Dudley, and Burroughs, Margaret. For
        Malcolm: Poems on the Life and Death of Malcolm
        X. Detroit: Broadside Press, 1969.

        A collection of poetry by various authors,
        dedicated to Malcolm.

2-28   Rose, Shirley. Promises and Power: Myths of the
        Acquisition of Literacy. Ph.D. Dissertation:
        University of Southern California, 1984.

        A study of the patterns and processes of the acqui-
        sition of literacy, utilizing five autobiographies,
        including Malcolm's.

2-29   Rudzka, Ostyn. Oratory of Martin Luther King, Jr. and
        Malcolm X: A Study in Linguistic Stylistics. Ph.D.
        Dissertation: University of Rochester, 1972.

        Using various linguistic theories, the author
        compares the speaking styles of King and Malcolm.

2-30   Shepard, Ray. Autobiography of Malcolm X. Lincoln,
        Nebraska: Cliff Notes, 1973.

        Shortened and popularized version of the
        autobiography.

2-31   Sibeko, David. An Address on Malcolm X's Legacy to
        the Black Struggle in Azania and the U.S.A.
        Chicago: Workers Voice, 1979.

        This pamphlet, from a speech delivered by Sibeko,
        the former head of Pan-Africanist Congress of South
        Africa, finds Malcolm's most enduring legacy in his
        commitment to Pan-Africanism and in his opposition to
        imperialism.

2-32   T'Shaka, Oba. Political Legacy of Malcolm X.
        Chicago: Third World Press, 1983.

        The author finds that Malcolm's legacy to the Afro-
        American movement is the doctrine of Pan-Africanism.

Criticizes some interpreters of Malcolm, particularly
Marxists, for distorting Malcolm's comments and positions in his last year.

2-33   Tyler, Bruce. Black Radicalism in Southern Californ-
        ia, 1950-1982. Ph.D. Dissertation: University of
        California, Los Angeles, 1983.

        Focusing on the Los Angeles riots of the 1960s, the
        author points out the role of Malcolm and other Afro-
        American leaders in politicizing the Afro-American
        community, thus laying the precondition for the riots
        and the activism of the 1960s and 1970s.

2-34   Williams, Michael. Relationship between Nkrumahism
        and Twentieth Century Leftist Thought in the
        African World. Ph.D. Dissertation: Notre Dame
        University, 1981.

        An examination of the thought of Kwame Nkrumah and
        other African and Afro-American left-wing theorists,
        including Malcolm.

2-35   Wolfenstein, Eugene. The Victims of Democracy:
        Malcolm X and the Black Revolution. Berkeley:
        University of California Press, 1981.

        Using a combination of Marxism and Freudianism, the
        author examines Malcolm's life through the discipline
        of psychohistory. He views Malcolm's life as an
        example of an oppressed person coming into awareness
        of himself vis-à-vis his oppressor.

2-36   Wood, John. Humor as a Form of Political Action: The
        Case of Malcolm X. Ph.D. Dissertation: Arizona
        State University, 1975.

        Using written and recorded speeches, the author
        examines the uses of humor in Malcolm's speaking
        style.

                        JUVENILE LITERATURE

2-37   Adoff, Arnold. Malcolm X. New York: Crowell, 1970.

2-38   Curtis, Richard. The Life of Malcolm X.
         Philadelphia: McRea-Smith, 1971.

2-39   Haskins, James. Picture Life of Malcolm X. New York:
         Watts, 1975.

2-40   White, Florence. Malcolm X: Black and Proud. New
         Canaan, CT: Garrard, 1975.

III ARTICLES

3-1   Adegbalola, Gaye Todd. "A Conversation with Martin
        and Malcolm." Black Collegian 8:4 Jan-Feb 1978.

        Construct of a debate between Dr. King and Malcolm,
        using excerpts from the speeches and writings of each.
        Topics discussed include integration, nonviolence, and
        nationalism.

3-2   Allen, Robert. "Malcolm X: 2/21/65." Village Voice,
        17 Feb 1966, p. 5.

        Eyewitness account of the assassination.

3-3   Bailey, A. Peter. "A Selected Bibliography of Books
        and Articles Relating to the Life of Malcolm X," in
        Malcolm X: The Man and His Times (New York:
        Macmillan, 1969), p. 352.

        A short bibliography of Malcolm covering the major
        books and articles to 1969.

3-4   Bailey, A. P. "The Ties That Bind." Essence 12:78 Ja
        1982.

        Story of the two eldest daughters of Malcolm and
        Dr. King teaming up to produce and star in a play
        based upon their fathers' ideas.

3-5   Baldwin, James. "Letter from a Region in My Mind."
        New Yorker 38:59 17 Nov 1962.

        An essay in which Baldwin details his experiences
        within the Christian Church and offers comments, both

27

personal and philosophical, on his meetings and
relationship with Malcolm X and Elijah Muhammad.

3-6   Baldwin, James. "Malcolm and Martin." Esquire 77:94
        Apr 1972.

        An essay in which Baldwin relates his reactions to
        the assassinations of Malcolm and Dr. King. Includes
        some personal reminiscences and details his attempts
        to write a screenplay based on Malcolm's autobiograph-
        y. Concludes with a brief attempt at comparing the
        meanings of Malcolm and Martin.

3-7   Baraka, Amiri. "Malcolm X and Paul Robeson," in Amiri
        Baraka, Daggers and Javelins (New York: Morrow,
        1984), p. 263.

        Views Robeson and Malcolm as the two outstanding
        examples of anti-imperialists among Afro-Americans.
        Concludes that their legacy points toward the use of
        Marxism-Leninism as a philosophy for Afro-American
        liberation.

3-8   Bates, Eveline. "We'll Never Be the Same." American
        Dialog 1:23 Oct-Nov 1964.

        Article by a young white civil rights worker on her
        experiences during a summer spent in Mississippi. She
        evaluates all of the negative aspects of the summer,
        thinking that the racism of whites may vindicate
        Malcolm's ideas. She also points to a new spirit of
        interracialism that may triumph over racism.

3-9   Benson, Thomas. "Rhetoric and Autobiography: The Case
        of Malcolm X." Quarterly Journal of Speech 60:1
        Feb 1974.

        Argues that Malcolm's autobiography is a successful
        piece of rhetoric in the sense that he presented the
        changes in his life and philosophy in a coherent
        pattern.

3-10   Berthoff, Werner. "Witness and Testament: Two
        Contemporary Classics." New Literary History 2:311
        Wint 1971.

        This comparison of Malcolm's Autobiography with
        Norman Mailer's Armies of the Night views Malcolm's
        book as being in the vein of conversion narratives.
        Much attention is paid to the type of literary
        criticism that is applicable to this type of work.

3-11   "Bethune, Lebert. "Malcolm X in Europe," in Malcolm
        X: The Man and His Times (New York: Macmillan,
        1969), p. 266.

        An account of Malcolm's visit to France in 1964 and
        England in 1965. Author tells of meeting with Malcolm
        and describes his effect upon expatriate Americans and
        Africans in Paris.

3-12   Black, Pearl. "Malcolm X Returns." Liberator 5:5 Ja
        1965.

        Covers Malcolm's speech upon returning to New York
        from Africa. Includes his comments on the relation-
        ship of Africa to Afro-Americans and the reporter's
        sense of the crowd that gathered to hear and welcome
        Malcolm.

3-13   Boggs, James. "Beyond Malcolm X." Monthly Review
        29:30 Dec 1977.

        Author argues that revolutionaries must go beyond
        the thought of Malcolm X by using the method of
        dialectical materialism to find solutions to problems
        of a highly technological society.

3-14   Boggs, James. "The Influence of Malcolm X on the
        Political Consciousness of Black Americans," in
        Malcolm X: The Man and His Times (New York:
        Macmillan, 1969), p. 50.

        Boggs locates the conditions for Malcolm's influ-
        ence in the growing militancy sparked by the urban
        rebellions of the 1960s. Boggs goes on to point out

the weaknesses in traditional Marxist ideology and
advocates the development of a Black Revolution in the
U.S.

3-15   Borders, James. "Postscript on the Assassination of
        Malcolm X." Black Collegian 35:66 Dec 1980.

        Raises unanswered questions about the assassina-
        tion. Points out that FBI documents point to a
        possible government conspiracy behind the
        assassination.

3-16   Boulware, Marcus. "Minister Malcolm: Orator
        Profunda." Negro History Bulletin 30:12 Nov 1967.

        This article examines, in popular language, the
        speaking style of Malcolm and its great effectiveness.

3-17   Bradley, David. "My Hero, Malcolm X." Esquire
        100:488 Dec 1983.

        The author, an Afro-American novelist, explains
        Malcolm's popularity, in part, by the fact that he was
        one of the common people and could articulate their
        desires and frustrations.

3-18   Breitman, George. "Introduction." International
        Socialist Review 28:1 Mar-Apr 1967.

        A written introduction to Malcolm's speech on Afro-
        American history. The author gives the background in
        which the speech was given, locating it within
        Malcolm's plan to start a new organization.

3-19   Breitman, George. "Myths About Malcolm X: Two
        Views." International Socialist Review 28:43 Sept-
        Oct 1967.

        In this speech the author attempts to refute the
        points made by Albert Cleague (see 3-26). Includes a
        lengthy question and answer period in which the author
        discusses Malcolm and Marxism and how the book Malcolm
        X Speaks came to be published.

3-20   Campbell, Finley. "Voices of Thunder, Voices of Rage:
        A Symbolic Analysis of a Selection from Malcolm X's
        'Message to the Grass Roots.'" Speech Teacher
        14:101 Mar 1970.

        A symbolic action analysis of a portion of
        Malcolm's speech. Author focuses on analogies and
        symbolism to reflect Malcolm's fundamental views.

3-21   "Checklists of Change, the Civil Rights Drive: 1954-
        68." Senior Scholastic 93:8, 20 Sept 1968.

        Contains a brief biographical entry on Malcolm.

3-22   Clarke, John Henrik. "Introduction," in Malcolm X:
        The Man and His Times (New York: Macmillan, 1969),
        p. xiii.

        In this introduction Clarke gives a capsulized view
        of the life of Malcolm, highlighting the background of
        his political changes.

3-23   Clarke, John Henrik. "Malcolm X: The Man and His
        Times." Negro Digest 18:23 May 1969.

        Traces Malcolm's life through his political
        changes. Notes the fact that Malcolm's attempt to
        bring the Afro-American problem before the U.N. played
        a role in his assassination.

3-24   Clasby, Nancy. "Autobiography of Malcolm X: A Mythic
        Paradigm." Journal of Black Studies 5:18 Sept
        1974.

        This article views Malcolm's life, as chronicled in
        his autobiography, as following the pattern studied by
        Frantz Fanon in his works on colonial psychology.

3-25   Cleague, Albert. "Brother Malcolm," in Black Messiah
        by Albert Cleague (New York: Sheed and Ward, 1969).

        In this sermon Cleague draws parallels between
        Malcolm and Jesus Christ. He speaks mostly of

Malcolm's positions on black unity and on white people
as the enemy of Afro-Americans.

3-26   Cleague, Albert. "Malcolm X Myth." Liberator 7:4
        June 1967.

        The author attempts to dispose of the 'myth' that
        Malcolm was becoming an integrationist. He argues
        that black nationalists must begin to interpret
        Malcolm's teachings so that they will not be
        distorted.

3-27   Cleague, Albert. "Myths About Malcolm X," in Malcolm
        X: The Man and His Times (New York: Macmillan,
        1969), p. 13.

        In this speech, similar to but longer than the
        citation above, Cleague exposes the 'myths' that (1)
        Malcolm stopped viewing white people as the enemy, and
        (2) he tried to internationalize the Afro-American
        struggle. Cleague explains away many of Malcolm's
        comments as the sayings of a confused man facing
        certain death. He characterizes Malcolm's chief
        contribution as recognizing that integration is
        impossible and undesirable.

3-28   Cleague, Albert. "Myths About Malcolm X: Two
        Views." International Socialist Review 28:33 Sept-
        Oct 1967.

        Same as citation 3-26.

3-29   Cleaver, Eldridge. "Culture and Revolution: Their
        Synthesis in Africa." Black Scholar 3:32 Oct 1971.

        Reviews Malcolm's contribution toward relating the
        struggle of Afro-Americans to the struggle of
        Africans. Traces Malcolm's followers through two
        strands of thought, cultural nationalism and
        revolutionary nationalism. Argues for a synthesis of
        culture and revolutionary socialism.

3-30   Cleaver, Eldridge. "Letter from Prison: On Malcolm
          X." Ramparts 5:24 Aug 1966.

        Cleaver writes of the reaction among prisoners to
        Malcolm's assassination. He views Malcolm as having
        had a special meaning for Afro-American prisoners
        because Malcolm had spent time in prison. He also
        notes the decline of the Nation of Islam since
        Malcolm's assassination.

3-31   Cleaver, Eldridge. "Muslim's Decline." Ramparts 5:
          10 Feb 1967.

        In this essay Cleaver makes the point that the
        decline of the Nation of Islam was largely due to the
        widespread notion that they were implicated in the
        assassination of Malcolm.

3-32   Coles, Robert. "What Can We Learn from the Life of
          Malcolm X?" Teachers College Record 67:564 May
          1966.

        Uses Malcolm's life as an example of the ability of
        people to grow and change. Cites this as a lesson for
        teachers and others who work with the disadvantaged.

3-33   Crawford, Marc. "Ominous Malcolm X Exits from the
          Muslims." Life 56:40, 20 Mar 1964.

        Article reporting Malcolm's split from the Nation
        of Islam. Includes some brief quotes from Malcolm on
        taxes, non-violence, the military, and separation.
        Also quotes Dr. King on Malcolm's prediction of racial
        violence.

3-34   Davis, John. "Chickens Still Coming Home to Roost,"
          Village Voice 26 Feb 1985, p. 40.

        A discussion of the legacy of Malcolm to the Afro-
        American movement. The author finds this legacy
        largely in the international concerns of the movement
        and in the desire for Afro-American unity.

3-35   Davis, Ossie. "Our Own Black Shining Prince."
        Liberator 5:7 Apr 1965.

        The text of Davis's eulogy to Malcolm X lauds
        Malcolm as being an inspiration to Afro-Americans.

3-36   Davis, Ossie. "Our Shining Black Prince," in Malcolm
        X: The Man and His Times, p. xi.

        Same as citation 3-35 above.

3-37   Davis, Ossie. "Why I Eulogized Malcolm X." Negro
        Digest 15:64 Feb 1966.

        Author explains that Malcolm epitomized black
        manhood, daring to say and express thoughts that
        others feel but are afraid to express.

3-38   Davis, Ossie. "Why I Eulogized Malcolm X," in Malcolm
        X: The Man and His Times (New York: Macmillan,
        1969), p. 128.

        Same as citation 3-37 above.

3-39   Diamond, Stanley. "The Apostate Muslim." Dissent
        12:193 Spr 1965.

        The author views Malcolm's murder as a political
        assassination. He attempts to show that Malcolm's
        changing views, especially about whites, forced the
        Nation of Islam to have him killed.

3-40   Demarest, David. "Autobiography of Malcolm X: Beyond
        Didacticism." CLA Journal 16:179 Dec 1972.

        Argues that Malcolm's autobiography appeals to
        whites because of its didacticism, and more
        importantly, because of its literary style.

3-41   Doudu, Cameron. "Malcolm X: Prophet of Harlem." Drum
        Magazine (Ghana Edition), Oct 1964.

        Not available for annotation.

Text of a radio address read in Ghana. The author
compares the notices in the Afro-American press to the
'ruling class' press. Finds that the Afro-American
press had a better understanding of Malcolm.

3-42
DuBois, Shirley Graham.   "The Beginning Not the End,"
    in Malcolm X: The Man and His Times (New York:
    Macmillan, 1969), p. 125.

3-43   Eakin, Paul. "Malcolm X and the Limits of
        Autobiography." Criticism 18:230 Sum 1976.

This article views Malcolm's autobiography through
the prism of various autobiographical forms. Emphasis
is on Malcolm's continual taking on and discarding
identities.

3-44   Elmessiri, Abdelwahab. "Islam as a Pastoral in the
        Life of Malcolm X," in Malcolm X: The Man and His
        Times (New York: Macmillan, 1969), p. 69.

This essay examines the effect of Islam on Malcolm
X. In particular, how the Islamic view of society
influenced Malcolm's vision of a just society.

3-45   Epps, Archie. "The Theme of Exile in Malcolm X's
        Harvard Speeches." Harvard Journal of Negro
        Affairs 2:40, #1, 1968.

An analysis of Malcolm's speeches at Harvard, each
one given at a different point in his political
evolution. He argues that the themes of exile and
return occupy a continuing place in Malcolm's
philosophy.

3-46   Essien-Udom, E. U. and Ruby M. "Malcolm X: An
        International Man," in Malcolm X: The Man and His
        Times (New York: Macmillan, 1969), p. 235.

The authors trace the ideological evolution of
Malcolm from black nationalism to internationalism,
which the authors identify as Pan-Africanism. They
pay particular attention to Malcolm's pilgrimage to

Mecca and to his experiences in Africa as turning
points in the evolution.

3-47   Flick, Hank. "A Question of Identity: Malcolm X's Use
           of Religious Themes as a Means for Developing a
           Black Identity." Negro Educational Review 31:140
           July-Oct 1980.

        Uses examples from Malcolm's speeches in order to
        demonstrate that Malcolm used religion as the basis
        for developing an Afro-American identity.

3-48   Flick, Hank. "Malcolm X and the Prison Walls of
           America." Negro Educational Review 30:21 Ja 1979.

        The author uses the analogy of prison and confine-
        ment to view Malcolm's writings and speeches.

3-49   Flick, Hank. "Malcolm X: The Destroyer and Creator of
           Myths." Journal of Black Studies 12:166 Dec 1981.

        Argues that Malcolm was successful in combating
        negative racial myths and creating positive racial
        myths in their place.

3-50   Gardner, Jigs. "Murder of Malcolm X." Monthly Review
           16:802 Apr 1965.

        This article cites Malcolm's positions on self-
        defense and revolution and concludes that Malcolm was
        only the beginning of a black working class
        revolutionary movement.

3-51   Gillespie, Marcia. "Getting Down." Essence 3:39 May
           1972.

        Editorial marking the second anniversary of Essence
        magazine. Mentions Malcolm's role in heightening
        black pride.

3-52   Glanville, Brian. "Malcolm X." New Statesman 67:901,
           12 June 1964.

Article viewing Malcolm's effect on race relations
and his stands on non-violence and racial separatism. Includes quotes from James Baldwin on Malcolm's
impact.

3-53   Goldman, Peter. "Malcolm X: An Unfinished Story."
        New York Times Magazine 19 Aug 1979, p. 28.

Article on Hayer's new allegations. Hayer gives
details of how he and four other members of the Nation
of Islam stalked Malcolm and planned the
assassination. Article also tells of William
Kunstler's, lawyer representing Hayer, attempts to re-
open an investigation of the assassination.

3-54   Goldman, Peter. "Malcolm X: Witness for the
        Prosecution," in Black Leaders of the Twentieth
        Century (Urbana: University of Illinois Press,
        1979), p. 305.

An assessment of Malcolm's life and his impact on
Afro-American thought. Concludes that Malcolm was
groping for a political ideology in his last year and
that his legacy consists chiefly of an attitude, or
stance, on racial questions.

3-55   Grant, Earl. "The Last Days of Malcolm X," in Malcolm
        X: The Man and His Times (New York: Macmillan,
        1969), p. 83.

This essay, written by one of Malcolm's followers,
gives a detailed account of the last thirteen days of
his life. It includes the firebombing of his house,
his assassination, and his funeral.

3-56   Griffin, John. "Ten Years Later, the Legend Grows:
        The Unsolved Mystery Murder of Malcolm X." Sepia
        24:18 Feb 1975.

Author retells the story of Malcolm's life, noting
that there is still little evidence to prove the
identity of his assassins.

3-57   Haley, Alex. "Alex Haley Remembers Malcolm X."
            Essence 14:52 Nov 1983.

        Relates the circumstances around the writing of
        Malcolm's autobiography. Compares Malcolm to Dr. King
        and gives some information on the children of Malcolm.

3-58   Hamilton, Bob. "El Hajj Malik Shabazz: Leader,
            Prophet, Martyr." Soulbook 1:81 Spr 1965.

        Argues that Malcolm left a legacy of militant
        nationalism that will continue to be a force among
        Afro-Americans.

3-59.   Harper, Frederick. The Influence of Malcolm X on
            Black Militancy." Journal of Black Studies 1:387
            June 1971.

        Views how Malcolm's personality traits, such as
        charisma, intelligence, and leadership, catapulted him
        into public prominence and affected an entire genera-
        tion of Afro-American activists. Specifically views
        Eldridge Cleaver and Stokely Carmichael as having been
        influenced by Malcolm.

3-60   Harper, Frederick. "A Reconstruction of Malcolm X's
            Personality." Afro-American Studies 3:1 June 1972.

        Analyzes several of Malcolm's personality traits
        that helped him attain a position of leadership in the
        Afro-American movement.

3-61   Hatch, Robert. "Racism and Religion: The Contrasting
            Views of Benjamin Mays, Malcolm X, and Martin
            Luther King, Jr." Journal of Religious Thought
            36:26 Fall-Wint 1979-80.

        Argues that Mays, King, and Malcolm all saw racism
        as the central problem in the U.S. and saw a relation
        between racism and the failures of the Christian
        church.

3-62   Henry, Lawrence. "Malcolm X." Now Mar-Apr 1966.

Not available for annotation.

3-63   Henry, Lawrence. "Malcolm X Lives." <u>Cavalier</u> June
       1966.

       Not available for annotation.

3-64   Hentoff, Nat. "Elijah in the Wilderness." <u>Reporter</u>
       23:37, 4 Aug 1960.

       This early article on the Nation of Islam focuses
       on their anti-white philosophy. Lengthy quotes are
       given from Malcolm, all expounding the Nation of
       Islam's philosophy.

3-65   Hentoff, Nat. "Remembering Malcolm." <u>Village Voice</u>,
       26 Feb 1985, p. 24.

       Personal recollections of the author's contacts as
       a journalist with Malcolm. Includes some speculation
       on the circumstances surrounding Malcolm's death.

3-66   Holt, Len. "Malcolm X the Mirror." <u>Liberator</u> 6:4 Feb
       1966.

       Author discusses ways to use the legacy of
       Malcolm. Finds Malcolm's most important ideas to be
       separation, Pan-Africanism, and black unity.

3-67   Holte, James. "Representative Voice: Autobiography
       and the Ethnic Experience." <u>Melus</u> 9:25 Summ 1982.

       Finds that Malcolm's autobiography fits squarely
       into an American tradition. Analyzes aspects such as
       conversion and change and relates it to the autobio-
       graphies of Piri Thomas and Constantine Panunzio.
       Concludes that ethnic autobiographies greatly enrich
       American literature.

3-68   Hoyt, Charles. "The Five Faces of Malcolm X." <u>Negro
       American Literature Forum</u> 4:107 Wint 1970.

Traces Malcolm's different identities from Malcolm
Little to El Hajj Malik El Shabazz.

3-69   Illo, John. "Rhetoric of Malcolm X." Columbia
        University Forum 9:5 Spr 1966.

Writer views Malcolm in the tradition of great
orators, speaking for justice and reason in an unjust
society.

3-70   Jones, Lisa Chapman. "Talking Book: Oral History of a
        Movement." Village Voice, 26 Feb 1985, p. 18.

Author believes that the best way to understand
Malcolm and his impact is through oral history. The
article contains excerpts of comments from several
people active in the OAAU, including Ella Collins,
Malcolm's sister. They speak of their personal con-
tact with Malcolm and about his influence on the Afro-
American community.

3-71   Kaminsky, Marc. "Radical Affirmatives." American
        Scholar 36:621 Aug 1967.

This article focuses on Malcolm, Jean Genet, and
Norman Mailer as inspired rebels confronting America.

3-72   Karenga, M. Ron. "Socio-Political Philosophy of
        Malcolm X." Western Journal of Black Studies 3:251
        Wint 1979.

In this article the author attempts to categorize
the essential theoretical components of Malcolm's
political philosophy. These include black nationalism, Pan-Africanism, Third World solidarity, and the
role of Islam.

3-73   Karenga, M. Ron. "Malcolm and the Messenger." Black
        News 4:4, #21, 1982.

Discussion of the split as a conflict between
radicals (Malcolm) and conservatives (Elijah Muhammad)
in the context of a growing Nation of Islam. Views

the FBI as having taken advantage of this to
assassinate Malcolm.

3-74   Karenga, M. Ron. "Malcolm X: His Significance and
        Legacy." Black News 4:30, #20, 1982.

        Discusses Malcolm's theoretical development and his
        ideas on Pan-Africanism, nationalism, and Third World
        Solidarity.

3-75   Kendrick, Curtis. "The Autobiography of Malcolm X."
        Journal of the National Medical Association 63:43
        Ja 1971.

        A study of Malcolm's autobiography. Draws
        parallels between Malcolm and the apostle Paul.

3-76   Kerina, Mburumba. "Malcolm X: The Apostle of
        Defiance--An African View" in Malcolm X: The Man
        and His Times (New York: Macmillan, 1969), p. 114.

        Author contends that Malcolm was representative of
        an "era of defiance" among black people world-wide.
        He views Malcolm's achievement as taking ideas from
        all revolutionary thinkers and welding them into an
        ideology for the liberation of blacks in Africa, the
        Caribbean, and the U.S.

3-77   Kgositsile, W. Keorapetse. "Brother Malcolm and the
        Black Revolution." Negro Digest 18:4 Nov 1968.

        Author cites the influence of Malcolm on black
        nationalism.

3-78   Kgositsile, W. Keorapetse. "Malcolm X and the Black
        Revolution: The Tragedy of a Dream Deferred" in
        Malcolm X: The Man and His Times, p. 43.

        This essay views the assassination of Malcolm X
        within the context of an attack upon radical Afro-
        American spokesmen.

3-79   Knebel, Fletcher. "Visit with the Widow of Malcolm
        X." Look 33:74, 4 Mar 1969.

        Describing a visit and interview with Betty
        Shabazz. She attempts to explain how Malcolm was
        misunderstood during his lifetime.

3-80   Krieg, Robert. "Malcolm X: Myth and Truthfulness:
        Journal of Religious Thought 36:37 Fall-Wint 1979-
        80.

        Author argues that Malcolm used myth to display
        truth by tracing Malcolm's religious beliefs from the
        Nation of Islam to orthodox Islam.

3-81   Lacy, Leslie Alexander. "Malcolm X in Ghana" in
        Malcolm X: The Man and His Times (New York:
        Macmillan, 1969), p. 217.

        Author relates Malcolm's two visits to Ghana.
        Included are Malcolm's interaction with students and a
        dispute between a news columnist in Ghana and Malcolm.

3-82   Laurino, Maro. "Who Were the Killers." Village
        Voice, 26 Feb 1985, p. 15.

        A discussion of the circumstances surrounding
        Malcolm's assassination. Author surveys some of the
        theories advanced and questions the role of the U.S.
        government in the assassination. Also questions the
        unwillingness of the government to reopen the trial.

3-83   Leiman, Melvin. "Malcolm X." Liberation 10:25 Apr
        1965.

        This article focuses on Malcolm's changing
        attitudes toward whites, his views on violence and
        self-defense, and his attitude toward capitalism and
        socialism.

3-84   Lincoln, C. Eric. "Meaning of Malcolm X" in Malcolm
        X: The Man and His Times (New York: Macmillan,
        1969), p. 7.

An assessment of the impact of Malcolm on Afro-
America. Includes some comments on Malcolm as a
martyr.

3-85   Lincoln, C. Eric. "Meaning of Malcolm X." Christian
        Century 82:431, 7 Apr 1965.

        Same as citation 3-84.

3-86   Lynch, Acklin. "America: The Meaning of Malcolm X."
        Black Collegian 11:38 Dec 1980-Ja 1981.

        Summation of Malcolm's life, based on the
        Autobiography.

3-87   MacInnes, Colin. "Malcolm, the Lost Hero." Negro
        Digest 16:4 May 1967.

        Finds heroism in Malcolm's intellectual and moral
        evolution.

3-88   Major, Clarence. "Malcolm the Martyr." Negro Digest
        16:37 Dec 1966.

        This essay is basically a personal memoir of the
        author's reaction to Malcolm. Includes remembrances
        of a speech Malcolm gave in Omaha in 1964 or 1965.
        The focus is on why the "power structure" had to
        assassinate Malcolm.

3-89   Mamiya, Lawrence. "From Black Muslim to Bilalian: The
        Evolution of a Movement." Journal for the
        Scientific Study of Religion 21:138 June 1982.

        Analyzes the changes in the Nation of Islam.
        Compares Malcolm's changed views with the changes
        introduced by Wallace Muhammad. Also compares Wallace
        Muhammad's American Muslim Mission with Louis
        Farrakhan's Nation of Islam on the basis of the social
        composition of their membership.

3-90   Mandel, Barrett. "Didactic Achievement in Malcolm X's
        Autobiography." Afro-American Studies 2:269 Mar
        1972.

        This article views Malcolm's autobiography as
        comparable to other spiritual-conversion writings.
        Locates it success in its didactic effect on the
        reader.

3-91   Martin, Abram. "Apartheid and Malcolm X." New Leader
        47:7, 22 June 1964.

        This article describes a meeting to protest
        apartheid and a speech by Malcolm (two separate
        events) at the University of Ibadan (Nigeria). The
        emphasis is on the audience reaction to Malcolm.

3-92   Massaquoi, Hans. "Mystery of Malcolm X." Ebony 19:38
        Sept 1964.

        Article points out that Malcolm may never be under-
        stood because of the many distortions about his
        beliefs in the media.

3-93   Mayfield, Julian. "Profile: Malcolm X: 1925-1965."
        African Review 1:9 May 1965.

        Not available for annotation.

3-94   Miller, Ross. "Autobiography as Fact and Fiction:
        Franklin, Adams, Malcolm X." Centennial Review
        16:221 Sum 1972.

        An essay exploring the structural and
        methodological factors defining autobiographical
        literature.

3-95   Moon, Henry. "Enigma of Malcolm X." Crisis 72:226
        Apr 1965.

        The author credits, or faults, the white media for
        creating Malcolm because he was "good copy." He goes
        on to point out that Malcolm was completely out of
        touch with the mainstream of Afro-American thought.

3-96   Moore, Louise. "When a Black Man Stood Up."
         Liberator 6:7 July 1966.

         Points out Malcolm's influence on the Afro-American
         movement, in particular, his constant stressing of the
         theme of unity.

3-97   Morgan, John. "Malcolm X's Murder." New Statesman
         69:310, 26 Feb 1965.

         Notes Malcolm's influence among the Afro-American
         and African intellectuals. Points out that Malcolm
         was killed just as he was moving closer to Dr. King.

3-98   Morrison, Allan. "Who Killed Malcolm X?" Ebony
         20:135 Oct 1965.

         Author raises unanswered questions about the
         assassination, including international implications,
         and questions about Malcolm's bodyguards.

3-99   Moses, Gil. "Simple Finally Speaks Out to the White
         Liberal about Malcolm." Liberator 6:15 Mar 1966.

         A poem describing the reaction of a common Afro-
         American to Malcolm's death.

3-100   Neal, Lawrence. "Malcolm X and the Conscience of
         Black America." Liberator 6:10 Feb 1966.

         The author explains Malcolm's influence on young
         Afro-Americans and artists. He views Malcolm's legacy
         as a growth in black consciousness among all Afro-
         Americans.

3-101   Neal, Lawrence. "A Reply to Bayard Rustin: The
         Internal Revolution." Liberator 5:6 July 1965.

         A critique of Rustin's article (see citation 3-
         120). Author accuses Rustin of lacking in black
         awareness.

3-102   Norden, Eric. "Who Killed Malcolm X?" Realist

      Not available for annotation.

3-103   Nower, Joyce. "Cleaver's Vision of America and the
      New White Radical: A Legacy of Malcolm X." Negro
      American Literature Forum 4:12 Mar 1970.

      Views Cleaver as a logical extension of Malcolm X.
      Uses the concept of self-determination to show the
      influence of Afro-American radicals on the under-
      standing held by white radicals.

3-104   O'Gara, James. "After Malcolm X." Commonweal 82:8,
      26 Mar 1965.

      States that the death of Malcolm does not mean the
      death of black militancy and nationalism. Sees these
      manifestations existing as long as racism exists.

3-105   Ohmann, Carol. "Autobiography of Malcolm X: A
      Revolutionary Use of the Franklin Tradition."
      American Quarterly 22:131 Sum 1970.

      The author draws comparisons between Malcolm's
      autobiography and Benjamin Franklin's autobiography.
      He shows that there were similarities in the way they
      explained their lives and the standards upon which
      they judged other men.

3-106   Parks, Gordon. "Malcolm X: The Minutes of Our Last
      Meeting" in Malcolm X: The Man and His Times, p.
      120.

      Notes from a meeting two days before the assassina-
      tion. Includes a scene at Malcolm's home with his
      wife and several followers the night of the
      assassination.

3-107   Parks, Gordon. "Violent End of a Man Called Malcolm
      X." Life 58:26 5 Mar 1965.

      Author mentions conversations with Malcolm shortly

before his death. Also mentions plans for revenge by
Malcolm's followers.

3-108   Perry, Bruce Frazier. "Malcolm X in Brief: A
          Psychological Perspective." Journal of
          Psychohistory 11:491 Spr 1984.

        This article, based on material from a forthcoming
biography, views the psychological development of
Malcolm in his youth. Using interviews with family
and acquaintances the author exposes many inaccuracies
contained in Malcolm's autobiography, particularly in
descriptions of his mother and father. The author
views Malcolm's rebellion as rooted in his conflicts
with Christianity and authority as a youth.

3-109   Phillips, Waldo, "Pied Piper of Harlem." Christian
          Century 81:422 1 Apr 1964.

        Suggests that Malcolm's call for self-defense will
provoke the violence he has predicted.

3-110   Plimpton, George. "Miami Notebook: Cassius Clay and
          Malcolm X." Harper's 228:54 June 1964.

        The author tells of an interview with Malcolm X in
which Malcolm discusses the civil rights movement,
religion, and his relationship and thoughts about
Cassius Clay.

3-111   Power, Jonathan. "Malcolm X: A Reassessment."
          Encounter 41:33 Sept 1973.

        The author points out the historical background of
Malcolm's rise to prominence. He includes comparisons
to Dr. King, later black power advocates, and cate-
gorizes five main areas of Malcolm's philosophy: (1)
separatism, (2) attitude to whites, (3) relationship
to Africa, (4) economic philosophy, and (5) political
tactics.

3-112   Protz, Roger. "Real Reason Why Malcolm X Went to
          Africa." Sepia 13:42 Oct 1964.

Author speculates that the real reason Malcolm went to Africa was to seek legitimacy for Afro-American Muslims in the eyes of Arabic Muslims.

3-113   Al Qualam.   "Death of Malcolm X."   *Al Qualam* 1:11, 1980.

Not available for annotation.

3-114   Al Qualam.   "Malcolm: His Brilliant and Anguished Life."   *Al Qualam* 1:6, 1980.

Not available for annotation.

3-115   Al Qualam.   "Who Assassinated Malcolm X"   *Al Qualam* 1:12, 1980.

Not available for annotation.

3-116   Revolutionary Action Movement.   "Why Malcolm X Died."   *Liberator* 5:9 Apr 1965.

This statement sees the U.S. government as responsible for the assassination. Argues that Malcolm's international activities were a threat to the U.S.

3-117   Robinson, Cedric.   "Malcolm Little as a Charismatic Leader."   *Afro-American Studies* 3:81 Sept 1972.

A psycho-historical approach is used to analyze Malcolm's personal development and his ascendency as an Afro-American leader.

3-118   Robinson, Patricia.   "Malcolm X, Our Revolutionary Son and Brother" in *Malcolm X: The Man and His Times*, p. 56.

An essay on Malcolm using the analogy of the son who rebels against the father.

3-119 Rogers, Raymond and Jimmie. "Evolution of the
       Attitude of Malcolm X toward Whites." Phylon
       64:108 June 1983.

       Through use of evaluative assertion analysis the
       authors find that Malcolm's views toward white people
       were changing but not in a clear-cut way. They
       situate these findings within the context of the
       Cleague-Breitman debate. See citations 3-18 and 3-26.

3-120 Rustin, Bayard, and Kahn, Tom. "Ambiguous Legacy of
       Malcolm X." Dissent 12:188 Spr 1965.

       The authors focus on Malcolm's relation to the
       lower class and draw parallels between Malcolm and
       Booker T. Washington.

3-121 Saxe, Janet. "Malik el Shabazz: A Survey of His
       Interpreters." Black Scholar 1:51 May 1970.

       Author critiques Breitman, Lomax, and Clarke's
       writings on Malcolm. Finds Breitman's work mis-
       representative of Malcolm's ideas on separatism,
       socialism, and religion. Lomax and Clarke are found
       to have a more accurate interpretation of Malcolm's
       philosophy. Concludes that Malcolm was not becoming
       an integrationist or a socialist in his last year.

3-122 Schroth, Raymond. "Malcolm X Is Alive." America
       116:594 22 Apr 1967.

       Short reflective article on how the publication of
       Malcolm's autobiography and Malcolm X Speaks should
       change public perceptions of Malcolm.

3-123 Schroth, Raymond. "Redemption of Malcolm X."
       Catholic World 205:346 Sept 1967.

       This article looks at Malcom's life from a
       religious point of view, noting his rise from sin to
       redemption.

3-124   Sears, Art. "Malcolm X and the Press" in <u>Malcolm X:</u>
        <u>The Man and His Times</u>, p. 106.

        This essay, written by an Afro-American journalist,
        relates his meetings, interviews, and personal
        reactions to Malcolm.

3-125   Seraille, William. "Assassination of Malcolm X: The
        View from Home and Abroad." <u>Afro-Americans in New</u>
        <u>York Life and History</u> 5:43 Ja 1981.

        This article views the reactions to Malcolm's death
        in four categories: those who saw him as an integra-
        tionist, a victim of violence, a confused but talented
        racist, and as a revolutionary martyr. Author relies
        on numerous articles and press clippings.

3-126   Seraille, William. "David Walker and Malcolm X:
        Brothers in Radical Thought." <u>Black World</u> 22:68
        Oct 1973.

        Draws parallels between Malcolm and David Walker
        around the issues of violence, black unity, and
        freedom.

3-127   Shabazz, Betty. "Legacy of My Husband, Malcolm X."
        <u>Ebony</u> 24:172 June 1969.

        Malcolm's widow briefly reviews his basic political
        views at the time of his death and gives many personal
        reminiscences of Malcolm as a husband.

3-128   Shabazz, Betty. "Malcolm X as a Husband and Father"
        in <u>Malcolm X: The Man and His Times</u>, p. 132.

        This essay gives a personal portrait of Malcolm.
        The author, Malcolm's widow, comments on their
        courtship, family life, and his interaction with their
        children.

3-129   Shapiro, Herbert. "The Education of Malcolm X."
        <u>Jewish Currents</u> 20:6 Oct 1966.

Not available for annotation.

3-130   Smith, A. Adeyemi. "Malcolm on Islam and Social
        Justice." African Mirror 3:41, July 1980.

        Not available for annotation.

3-131   Smith, Baxter. "FBI Memos Reveal Repression
        Schemes." Black Scholar 5:43 Apr 1974.

        The author cites released FBI memos to show that
        there was a government conspiracy to destroy the Afro-
        American movement. Mentions government surveillance of
        Malcolm and questions about his assassination.
        Concludes with a demand for a Black Commission of
        Inquiry into these cases.

3-132   Smith, Baxter. "New Evidence of FBI 'Disruption
        Program'." Black Scholar 6:43 July-Aug 1975.

        Author details Malcolm's relationship to the
        Socialist Workers Party and cites government attempts
        to sabotage it. Quotes FBI memos citing a fear of
        Marxist ideas in the Afro-American movement.

3-133   Snellings, Roland. "Malcolm X as International
        Statesman." Liberator 6:6 Feb 1966.

        Written in poetic prose, a tribute to Malcolm X
        focusing on his relations abroad as a spokesman for
        Afro-America.

3-134   Southwick, Albert. "Malcolm X: Charismatic
        Demagogue." Christian Century 5 June 1963.

        Article based upon an interview with Malcolm.
        Author concludes that the Nation of Islam challenges
        Christianity to deal with the racial problem
        effectively.

3-135   Spellman, A. B. "Legacy of Malcolm X." Liberator
        5:11 June 1965.

Argues for a new organization based on Malcolm's political philosophy.

3-136   Spitz, Barry.   "The End of Malcolm X."   Sepia 14:14
        May 1965.

Author surveys the circumstances of Malcolm's assassination, suggesting irony in the fact that he was killed in Harlem by Afro-Americans.

3-137   Strickland, William.   "The Last Real Social Critic."
        Village Voice, 26 Feb 1985, p. 15.

Survey of the era in which Malcolm lived.   Author concludes that the U.S. has no leader with the moral authority that Malcolm had.

3-138   Sykes, Ossie.   "The Week that Malcolm X Died."
        Liberator 5:4 Apr 1965.

Author describes Harlem following the assassination.   Included is a description of the funeral and burial.

3-139   Sykes, Ossie, and Wilson, Charles E.   "Malcolm X: A
        Tragedy of Leadership."   Liberator 5:7 May 1965.

Views the tragedy of Malcolm as the fact that he didn't have the time to fully develop himself once he left the Nation of Islam.

3-140   Thomas, Norman.   "Tragedy of Malcolm X."   America
        112:303, 6 Mar 1965.

Suggests that people should learn the futility of hate as shown through the life of Malcolm.

3-141   Thomas, Tony.   "Malcolm X: His Strategy for Black
        Liberation."   International Socialist Review 32:28
        May 1971.

Using quotations from Malcolm's speeches, the author sets out Malcolm's views on black nationalism, imperialism, organization, and alliances.

3-142   Vernon, Robert. "Malcolm X: Voice of the Black
        Ghetto." International Socialist Review 26:36 Spr
        1965.

        Focuses on Malcolm's changing politics in his last
        year. The author analyzes these changes within the
        context of new currents within the civil rights
        movement.

3-143   Walker, Wyatt. "Nothing But a Man." Negro Digest
        14:29 Aug 1965.

        Finds the meaning of Malcolm X in his symbolization
        of black manhood. Contains a comparison of Malcolm X
        and Martin Luther King.

3-144   Walker, Wyatt. "Nothing But a Man" in Malcolm X: The
        Man and His Times (New York: Macmillan, 1969), p.
        64.

        Same as citation 3-143.

3-145   Warde, William. "Life and Death of Malcolm X."
        International Socialist Review 26:35 Spr 1965.

        This article focuses on the development of
        Malcolm's political philosophy in his last year. The
        author makes note of the potential Malcolm had for
        redirecting the civil rights movement.

3-146   Warren, Robert Penn. "Malcolm X: Mission and
        Meaning." Yale Review 56:167 Wint 1967.

        Brief review of Malcolm's life, assassination, and
        impact. Author speculates on Malcolm's role in the
        civil rights movement had he lived.

3-147   Watts, Daniel. "The Last Spokesman." Liberator 6:3
        Feb 1966.

        Views Malcolm as the most articulate spokesman of
        the Afro-American people. Argues that now is the time
        to focus on building organizations that will survive
        charismatic leaders.

3-148   Watts, Daniel. "Malcolm X: The Unfulfilled
        Promise." Liberator 5:3 Mar 1965.

        This editorial argues against fratricidal warfare
        and for Afro-American unity against racism.

3-149   Watts, Daniel, "Malcolm X vs. White Press." Liberator
        6:3 Mar 1966.

        Author is critical of press coverage of a memorial
        march held in honor of Malcolm.

3-150   Wechsler, James. "Cult of Malcolm X." Progressive
        28:24 June 1964.

        Author criticizes Malcolm for his anti-white views.
        Includes a personal report of a speech Malcolm gave at
        a meeting sponsored by the Socialist Workers Party.

3-151   Wechsler, James. "Why Malcolm X Quit the Black
        Muslims." Sepia 13:58 May 1964.

        Author describes the reasons that Malcolm left the
        Nation of Islam. Views the most important reason as
        jealousy between some of Elijah Muhammad's sons and
        Malcolm.

3-152   Weiss, Samuel. "Ordeal of Malcolm X." South Atlantic
        Quarterly 76:497 Aut 1977.

        This article essentially traces Malcolm's life. It
        provides a good brief summary of Malcolm's
        autobiography.

3-153   White, Butch. "Remembrance." Black World 24:88 May
        1975.

        Short one-line vignettes by the author about
        Malcolm.

3-154   White, Milton. "Malcolm X in the Military." Black
        Scholar 1:31 May 1970.

Background of the founding of the Malcolm X
Association, a black cultural awareness group
comprised of U.S. military personnel. Author details
the resistance of the U.S. Army bureaucracy to its
founding.

3-155   Whitfield, Stephen. "Three Masters of Impression
        Management: Benjamin Franklin, Booker T.
        Washington, and Malcolm X as Autobiographers."
        South Atlantic Quarterly 77:399 Aut 1978.

        The author attempts to compare the autobiographies
        of these three men through the prism of "impression
        management." That is, their attempt to convey a
        certain image of themselves.

3-156   Wiley, Charles. "Who Was Malcolm X." National Review
        17:239, 23 Mar 1965.

        Comments on the author's meeting with Malcolm and
        discusses Malcolm's political philosophy, including
        his views on world revolution.

3-157   Williams, Robert F. "Malcolm X: Death Without
        Silence." Crusader 6:8 Mar 1965.

        Short note predicting that Afro-Americans will
        rally around Malcolm's ideas, in spite of his death.

3-158   Wilson, Charles E. "Leadership: Triumph in Leadership
        Tragedy," in Malcolm X: The Man and His Times, p.
        27.

        This essay views Malcolm's leadership in an
        organizational context, including the Nation of Islam,
        the OAAU, and his role in international affairs.

3-159   Wilson, Charles E. "Quotable Mr. X." Liberator 5:11
        May 1965.

        An assemblage of quotes by Malcolm on such topics
        as white America, Afro-America, Africa, and black
        nationalism.

3-160   Winfrey, Charles.   "The Evolution of Malcolm X: From
        Poseur to Pan-Africanist."   Mazungumzo 2:74 #3,
        1972.

        Traces Malcolm's political evolution from his days
        as a criminal to his founding of the OAAU. Views the
        height of Malcolm's achievement as his belief in Pan-
        Africanism and his opposition to imperialism.

IVA NEWS REPORTS--MAINSTREAM PRESS

4A-1   "City College President Clears Appearance by Malcolm
        X." New York Times, 23 Nov 1961, p. 50.

        Story of Malcolm X's scheduled appearance on a
        panel entitled "Academic Freedom and the Ban"
        sponsored by the Eugene V. Debs Club of the City
        College of New York. (120)

4A-2   "Three in Speech-ban Controversies Appear at City
        College Meetings." New York Times, 8 Dec 1961, p.
        28.

        News item on a series of speakers, including
        Malcolm X, at the City College of New York. (200)

4A-3   "Mayor Yorty Says Cult Backs Hate." New York Times,
        27 July 1962, p. 8.

        Lists charges and counter-charges between Malcolm X
        and Samuel Yorty, Mayor of Los Angeles, concerning the
        killing of a member of the Nation of Islam by the Los
        Angeles police. (235)

4A-4   "Muslim May Join Englewood Anti-Segregation Drive."
        New York Times, 5 Aug 1962, p. 55.

        Story of a civil rights leader in Englewood, N.J.
        who invited Malcolm X to address an anti-segregation
        rally. (410)

4A-5   "Muslim Charges Englewood Sham." New York Times, 6
        Aug 1962, p. 27.

Story of Malcolm's acceptance of an invitation to
speak at an anti-segregation rally. Gives Malcolm's
reasons why he accepted.

4A-6   "Negro Pupils Used as Pawns, Englewood Protest Group
         Says." New York Times, 7 Aug 1962, p. 18.

         Gives background on the Englewood dispute. Lists
         reactions of several Afro-American leaders to the
         Malcolm X invitation. (410)

4A-7   "Malcolm X Decides Not to Speak at Protest Rally in
         Englewood." New York Times, 8 Aug 1962, p. 63.

         Lists Malcolm's reasons for canceling the speaking
         engagement. Includes statements by Afro-American
         leaders opposed to Malcolm speaking. (600)

4A-8   "Muslims on Coast Fight Riot Case." New York Times,
         26 Aug 1962, p. 64.

         Gives information on a disturbance between Muslims
         and Los Angeles police on April 27, 1962. Includes
         statements by Afro-American leaders on the Nation of
         Islam and on Malcolm X. (1000)

4A-9   "Muslims Press Race Separation--Malcolm X at Chicago
         Rally." New York Times, 28 Feb 1963, p. 5.

         Story on the annual convention of the Nation of
         Islam. Includes lengthy quotes from Malcolm's speech
         demanding a separate state and calling for united
         action among Afro-American organizations. (800)

4A-10   "Assertive Spirit Stirs Negroes." New York Times, 23
         Apr 1963, p. 20.

         Cites increasing militancy and nationalism in the
         Afro-American community. Lengthy discussion of the
         Nation of Islam and Malcolm X, with comments from
         Afro-American leaders and scholars. (4000)

4A-11 "Powell Sees Race Riot in Capital Unless Conditions
        Are Improved." New York Times, 6 May 1963, p. 59.

        Report of a speech by Adam C. Powell in which he
        states that Malcolm X will be moving to Washington,
        D.C. (400)

4A-12 "Malcolm X Starting Drive in Washington." New York
        Times, 10 May 1963, p. 1.

        On Malcolm's move to Washington, D.C. Includes
        lengthy excerpts of statements by Malcolm giving his
        rationale and goals for moving. (650)

4A-13 "Malcolm X Terms Dr. King's Tactics Futile." New York
        Times, 11 May 1963, p. 9.

        On Malcolm's arrival in Washington, D.C. Includes
        comments by Malcolm on the leadership of the Civil
        Rights Movement and the demonstrations in Birmingham.
        (600)

4A-14 "Newsman Beaten After Rally Here." New York Times, 15
        May 1963, p. 26.

        On an anti-segregation rally addressed by Malcolm X
        and Dr. M. L. King's brother. (500)

4A-15 "Malcolm X Scores Kennedy on Racial Policy." New York
        Times, 17 May 1963, p. 14.

        Article based on an interview after a meeting
        between Malcolm X and an unidentified member of
        Congress. Contains lengthy quotes from Malcolm
        critical of President Kennedy's handling of civil
        rights issues. (500)

4A-16 "Why Black Muslims Are Focusing on the Nation's
        Capital Now." U.S. News and World Report, 27 May
        1963, p. 24.

        On Malcolm's move to Washington, D.C. Includes his
        comments on Muslim activities in the area and his
        demand for a separate state. (650)

4A-17   "Malcolm X Disputes Non-Violence Policy." New York
        Times, 5 June 1963, p. 29.

        Report of a television interview in which Malcolm
        accuses Dr. King of disarming Afro-Americans through
        his policy of non-violence. (200)

4A-18   "Dr. King Attacks Kennedy Record." New York Times, 10
        June 1963, p. 20.

        In the context of a lengthy article on Dr. King,
        the reporter mentions a criticism Malcolm made against
        Adam C. Powell. (50)

4A-19   "Malcolm X Tells Rally in Harlem, Kennedy Fails to
        Help Negroes." New York Times, 30 June 1963, p. 45.

        Report of a speech wherein Malcolm criticizes
        Kennedy for his interest in European problems and
        disinterest in Afro-American problems. (400)

4A-20   "Enter Muhammad?" National Review 2 July 1963, p. 19.

        Editorial in which the author admits that the
        Nation of Islam is one of the few Afro-American
        organizations with a concrete program. (500)

4A-21   "Malcolm Assails Racial Integration." New York Times,
        14 July 1963, p. 50.

        Report of a speech by Malcolm, at a Harlem rally,
        in which he argues the futility of integration and
        demands a separate state. (100)

4A-22   "Brooklyn Rally Held by Muslims." New York Times, 28
        July 1963, p. 44.

        Report of a rally in which Malcolm calls for unity
        among all Afro-American organizations. Includes his
        comments on non-violence, Dr. King, and white
        participation in civil rights demonstrations. (450)

4A-23 "Church to Enlist Catholics Here for Capital Civil
       Rights Rally." New York Times, 11 Aug 1963, p. 1.

       In the context of an article on preparations for
       the March on Washington, mentions a rally held in
       Harlem in which Malcolm called for a 'united black
       front.' (250)

4A-24 "Koran's Lesson." New York Times Magazine, 15 Sept
       1963, p. 40.

       Letter to the editor from a Turkish Muslim
       disputing Malcolm's racial interpretation of Islam.
       (75)

4A-25 "Bunche Upbraids Race Extremists." New York Times, 24
       Oct 1963, p. 25.

       Report of a speech by Ralph Bunche in which he
       criticizes 'race extremists,' including Malcolm, for
       suggesting that equality is unattainable. (500)

4A-26 "Malcolm X Scores U.S. and Kennedy." New York Times,
       2 Dec 1963, p. 21.

       Report of a speech in New York in which Malcolm
       comments on Kennedy's assassination, the March on
       Washington, and Kennedy's record on civil rights
       issues. (350)

4A-27 "Malcolm X Silenced for Remarks on Assassination of
       Kennedy." New York Times, 5 Dec 1963, p. 22.

       Report of Malcolm's suspension as spokesman for the
       Nation of Islam. Includes comments from Elijah
       Muhammad, Malcolm (including his criticism of the
       press for distorting his comments), and reports of
       dissension within the Nation of Islam. (400)

4A-28 "Malcolm Expected to Be Replaced." New York Times, 6
       Dec 1963, p. 27.

Reports a rumor that Malcolm would be replaced as
Minister of the New York Mosque. (200)

4A-29 "X on the Spot." Newsweek, 16 Dec 1963, p. 27.

On Malcolm's comments on Kennedy's assassination
and on his suspension as national spokesman for the
Nation of Islam. (300)

4A-30 "Black Muslims Asked to Help Treat Addicts Here." New
       York Times, 10 Ja 1964, p. 85.

On the Nation of Islam's techniques for drug
rehabilitation. Mentions Malcolm's narcotics
background. (650)

4A-31 "Malcolm X's Role Dividing Muslims." New York Times,
       26 Feb 1964, p. 34.

On dissension within the Nation of Islam. Sees its
basis on Malcolm's attempt to bring the Muslims into a
more activist political role. (600)

4A-32 "Malcolm Absent as Muslims Meet." New York Times, 27
       Feb 1964, p. 23.

Report on the Nation of Islam's annual convention.
Notes the absence of Malcolm and New York Muslims.
Speculates on an internal power struggle. (450)

4A-33 "Clay Talks with Malcolm X Here." New York Times, 2
       Mar 1964, p. 36.

Report of a meeting between Cassius Clay and
Malcolm. (120)

4A-34 "Clay Tells of Plans to Visit Mecca." New York Times,
       5 Mar 1964, p. 39.

Report of a tour of the United Nations by Clay and
Malcolm. (350)

4A-35   "Malcolm X Splits with Muhammad." New York Times, 9
         Mar 1964, p. 1.

         Report of the split. Includes lengthy quotes from
         Malcolm on his plans to form a black nationalist
         group, become involved in the civil rights movement,
         and spread the idea of self-defense. (700)

4A-36   "Malcolm X Sees Rise in Violence." New York Times, 13
         Mar 1964, p. 20.

         Report on a press conference. Includes Malcolm's
         ideas on self-defense and school integration. (500)

4A-37   "To Arms with Malcolm X." New York Times, 14 Mar
         1964, p. 22.

         Editorial denouncing Malcolm's position on self-
         defense. (120)

4A-38   "Negroes Ponder Malcolm's Move." New York Times, 15
         Mar 1964, p. 46.

         Reaction on Malcolm's new direction from Afro-
         American leaders. Includes comments by Bayard Rustin,
         James Foreman, Gloria Richardson, and Whitney Young.
         (750)

4A-39   "Dr. King Urges Non-Violence in Rights Protests." New
         York Times, 15 Mar 1964, p. 46.

         Includes King's comments critical of Malcolm's
         position on self-defense. Notes King's plans to meet
         with Malcolm. (300)

4A-40   "Murphy Says City Will Not Permit Rights Violence."
         New York Times, 16 Mar 1964, p. 1.

         Report of a speech by the New York City Police
         Commissioner in which he accuses Malcolm and others of
         attempting to incite violence. (700)

4A-41 "Leaders Crowd into Spotlight at Galamison's
         Headquarters." New York Times, 17 Mar 1964, p. 25.

         Report on the scene at the headquarters of a New
         York City school boycott. Mentions Malcolm's
         interaction with the crowd and leaders of the boycott.
         (500)

4A-42 Malcolm X in Traffic Court, Denies Speeding on
         Bridge." New York Times, 17 Mar 1964, p. 18.

         News item on Malcolm's appearance in traffic court.
         (100)

4A-43 "1,000 in Harlem Cheer Malcolm X." New York Times, 23
         Mar 1964, p. 18.

         Report on Malcolm's first mass rally. Includes
         quotes from Malcolm on a black nationalist political
         party, voting power, and internationalizing the Afro-
         American struggle. (250)

4A-44 "Malcolm's Brand X." Newsweek, 23 Mar 1964, p. 32.

         Article on Malcolm's split from the Nation of
         Islam. Includes quotes and references to his
         positions on self-defense, a black political party,
         and integration. (1500)

4A-45 "Brother Malcolm: His Theme Now Is Violence." U.S.
         News and World Report, 23 Mar 1964, p. 19.

         Report on Malcolm's split from the Nation of
         Islam. Focuses on his call for self-defense. (300)

4A-46 "Malcolm X Backs House Rights Bill." New York Times,
         27 Mar 1964, p. 10.

         Reports Malcolm's support for the Civil Rights Act.
         (100)

4A-47 "Black Muslims." Times (London), 30 Mar 1964, p. 9.

Notes that Malcolm's entry into the Afro-American movement may challenge the trend towards integration. (600)

4A-48   "Pied Piper of Harlem." Christian Century, 1 Apr
        1964, p. 422.

        Editorial criticizing Malcolm's statements calling
        on Afro-Americans to arm themselves and form rifle
        clubs. (200)

4A-49   "Malcolm X Plans Muslim Crusade." New York Times, 3
        Apr 1964, p. 23.

        Report of a speech Malcolm delivered to an
        organization of Christian ministers. He explains his
        plans to become an 'evangelist' of black nationalism.
        (500)

4A-50   "Muslim Code." New York Times Magazine, 5 Apr 1964,
        p. 60.

        Letter to the editor expressing positive aspects of
        the moral code of the Nation of Islam. (150)

4A-51   "Brutality Cases Urged for Study." New York Times, 7
        Apr 1964, p. 24.

        In an article on police brutality, Malcolm is
        reported to have spoken to a group of Afro-American
        ministers. (250)

4A-52   "Negro Moderation Decried by Malcolm X in Lebanon."
        New York Times, 2 May 1964, p. 56.

        News item on a speech delivered by Malcolm X in
        Lebanon. (100)

4A-53   "Malcolm X Pleased by Whites' Attitude on Trip to
        Mecca." New York Times, 8 May 1964, p. 1.

Report of a letter Malcolm wrote to a friend after his visit to Mecca. Describes his changing attitudes towards whites as a result of his visit. (600)

4A-54   "Malcolm X Feels 'At Home' in Africa." New York Times, 13 May 1964, p. 17.

Report of a press conference in Ghana. Malcolm describes his reactions to Africa and compares the U.S. to South Africa. (125)

4A-55   "Clay Makes Malcolm Ex-Friend." New York Times, 18 May 1964, p. 40.

Encounter between Clay and Malcolm in Ghana. Includes the text of a note Malcolm sent to Clay asking him to behave 'responsibly.' Includes Clay's response. (600)

4A-56   "Malcolm X Woos Two Rights Leaders." New York Times, 19 May 1964, p. 28.

Report of a letter Malcolm sent to Bayard Rustin and Milton Galaminson apologizing for past attacks and proposing united action. (150)

4A-57   "Warrant for Malcolm as Speeder Is Issued." New York Times, 20 May 1964, p. 33.

News item about a warrant issued for Malcolm. Notes that he was in Africa at the time of his court date. (100)

4A-58   "Malcolm Says He Is Backed Abroad." New York Times, 22 May 1964, p. 22.

Report of a press conference upon Malcolm's return to the U.S. He is reported as claiming support from several African nations for his plan to bring the Afro-American problem to the United Nations. (300)

4A-59 "Malcolm Regrets Race Separation." New York Times, 24
          May 1964, p. 61.

          Story of a debate between Malcolm and Louis Lomax
          in which Malcolm explains his new views on separation
          and integration. (250)

4A-60 "Six Malcolm X Followers Questioned by Police." New
          York Times, 17 June 1964, p. 34.

          News item of an incident between some of Malcolm's
          followers and several members of the Nation of Islam.
          (100)

4A-61 "Police on Alert over Muslim Rift." New York Times,
          18 June 1964, p. 25.

          About a confrontation between Malcolm's followers
          and members of the Nation of Islam. Includes both
          group's versions of the incident and voices fears over
          more confrontation. (500)

4A-62 "Negro Leaders Hail Passage [of Civil Rights Act]."
          New York Times, 20 June 1964, p. 1.

          Reaction of Afro-American leaders to the Civil
          Rights Act. Responses from Dr. King, James Farmer,
          and Malcolm. Malcolm expresses pessimism. (700)

4A-63 "Malcolm X Calls for Muslim Peace." New York Times,
          27 June 1964, p. 9.

          Reports on an open letter from Malcolm to Elijah
          Muhammad calling on both organizations to cease
          fighting and work together with other Afro-American
          organizations. (150)

4A-64 "NAACP Bids U.S. Rule Mississippi." New York Times,
          27 June 1964, p. 10.

          Coverage of an NAACP convention, which Malcolm
          attended. Mentions Malcolm's plans to start a new
          organization, the Afro-American Unity Party. (1000)

4A-65   "Elijah Muhammad Rallies His Followers in Harlem."
        New York Times, 29 June 1964, p. 1.

        Report of a rally held in Harlem by the Nation of
        Islam ostensibly held to offset defections among the
        Muslims to Malcolm. Contains some oblique references
        to Malcolm by Muhammad. (800)

4A-66   "Malcolm X Repeats Call for Negro Unity on Rights."
        . New York Times, 29 June 1964, p. 32.

        Reports a speech by Malcolm to the newly formed
        Organization of Afro-American Unity. He is quoted as
        calling for unity between the OAAU and the Nation of
        Islam through participation in the civil rights
        movement. (100)

4A-67   "Malcolm Says Muhammad Fails Cause of Negroes." New
        York Times, 30 June 1964, p. 20.

        Report of an interview in which Malcolm criticizes
        Muhammad for not becoming involved in the civil rights
        movement. (100)

4A-68   "Six Black Nationalists Indicted as Result of Clash in
        Harlem." New York Times, 4 July 1964, p. 7.

        Story of indictments against several of Malcolm's
        followers as the result of a confrontation with
        members of the Nation of Islam. (300)

4A-69   "Malcolm X to Meet Leaders of Africa." New York
        Times, 10 July 1964, p. 26.

        Reports Malcolm's departure to attend the
        Organization of African Unity meeting in Cairo. (100)

4A-70   "Malcolm X Predicts Bloodbath." Times (London), 11
        July 1964, p. 7.

        Reports Malcolm's arrival in London on his way to
        Cairo. (50)

NEWS REPORTS--MAINSTREAM PRESS   69

4A-71 "Malcolm X, in Cairo, Says He'll See African
       Leaders." New York Times, 14 July 1964, p. 23.

       On Malcolm's presence at the OAU meeting. Mentions
       his plan to seek the support of African leaders in
       bringing the Afro-American problem to the U.N. (75)

4A-72 "Malcolm X Bids Africans Take Negro Issue to U.N."
       New York Times, 18 July 1964, p. 2.

       Reports a statement circulated by Malcolm at the
       OAU meeting in Cairo. (100)

4A-73 "Malcolm X Lays Harlem Riot to 'Scare Tactics' of
       Police." New York Times, 21 July 1964, p. 22.

       On a statement by Malcolm (in Cairo) on the Harlem
       Riot. (100)

4A-74 "Black Nationalist Headquarters of Malcolm X
       Raided." New York Times, 24 July 1964, p. 8.

       In a longer article on the Harlem Riot this report
       mentions a raid by New York City policemen on the
       headquarters of the OAAU. Reportedly several weapons
       were seized. (50)

4A-75 "Rockefeller Hits News Restraints." New York Times, 5
       Aug 1964, p. 16.

       On a speech by New York Governor Nelson Rockefeller
       in which, among other points, he states that Malcolm's
       popularity exists only because of the media portrayal
       of him as a hero. (400)

4A-76 "Organizations and Leaders Campaigning for Negro Goals
       in the U.S." New York Times, 10 Aug 1964, p. 16.

       Short profiles of organizations and leaders in the
       civil rights movement, including Malcolm X. (250)

4A-77 "Malcolm X Seeks U.N. Negro Debate." New York Times,
       13 Aug 1964, p. 22.

       On Malcolm's activities in Cairo at the OAU
       meeting. Includes long excerpts from a statement
       Malcolm circulated there and mentions U.S. State
       Department interest in Malcolm's activities. (800)

4A-78 "Malcolm X Attacks U.S." New York Times, 23 Aug 1964,
       p. 86.

       On a statement Malcolm X made in Cairo accusing the
       U.S. of racism. (60)

4A-79 "Malcolm Ordered to Move from Black Muslim House."
       New York Times, 3 Sept 1964, p. 16.

       On a suit filed by the Nation of Islam to reclaim
       Malcolm's house. (100)

4A-80 "Malcolm X Article Favors Goldwater." New York Times,
       8 Sept 1964, p. 19.

       Report of an article by Malcolm in which he states
       that Goldwater might be the best candidate for Afro-
       Americans because he would dispel false illusions
       fostered by Johnson. (200)

4A-81 "Lesson of Malcolm X." Saturday Evening Post, 12 Sept
       1964, p. 84.

       Editorial in which the appearance of a Malcolm X is
       blamed on the tyranny of U.S. racism. Warns that if
       these injustices are not corrected Malcolm may be suc-
       ceeded by even 'weirder and more virulent' leaders.
       (350)

4A-82 "White New Yorkers Queried in Poll Say Rights Drive
       Has Gone Too Far." New York Times, 21 Sept 1964,
       p. 26.

       Lengthy story on a poll taken to measure racial
       attitudes among white New Yorkers. Mentions Malcolm
       having a disapproval rating of 60%. (25)

4A-83 "FBI Says Riots Had No Pattern or Single Leader." New
       York Times, 27 Sept 1964, p. 1.

       On an FBI report on the Harlem Riots. Briefly
       mentions Malcolm for comments on forming rifle clubs.
       (1000)

4A-84 "Malcolm Rejects Racist Doctrine." New York Times, 4
       Oct 1964, p. 59.

       Concerning a letter Malcolm wrote from Mecca in
       which he denounces Elijah Muhammad, black racism, and
       professes a belief in the brotherhood of man.
       Contains lengthy excerpts from the letter. (600)

4A-85 "Malcolm X Reports He Now Represents World Muslim
       Unit." New York Times, 11 Oct 1964, p. 13.

       On a letter Malcolm sent from Mecca announcing his
       appointment as the U.S. representative of the World
       Muslim League. (350)

4A-86 "Johnson Criticized." New York Times, 24 Oct 1964, p.
       28.

       Letter to the editor criticizing Pres. Lyndon
       Johnson for not condemning Malcolm X as he did the
       John Birch Society. (35)

4A-87 "Malcolm's Plan Irks Muslims Here." New York Times, 8
       Nov 1964, p. 48.

       Reports the reaction of the New York spokesman for
       the Nation of Islam to Malcolm. He criticizes Malcolm
       for denouncing Elijah Muhammad and faults him for
       attempting to inject black nationalism into the Nation
       of Islam. (450)

4A-88 "Malcolm X, Back in U.S., Accuses Johnson on Congo."
       New York Times, 25 Nov 1964, p. 17.

       Report of a statement made by Malcolm upon his
       return to the U.S. criticizing Johnson for his support
       of Tshombe. (100)

4A-89   "Malcolm X Exhorts Negroes to Look to African
         Culture." New York Times, 13 Dec 1964, p. 80.

         Report of a speech delivered to domestic peace
         corps workers. Malcolm discusses the role of Africa
         in Afro-American consciousness and defends his
         position on self-defense. Reporter describes the
         audience and their reaction. (400)

4A-90   "Malcolm Favors a Mau Mau in U.S." New York Times, 21
         Dec 1964, p. 20.

         Report of a speech given in Harlem, in support of
         the Mississippi Freedom Democratic Party, in which
         Malcolm discusses the need for self-defense. (500)

4A-91   "Malcolm X Cites Role in U.N. Fight." New York Times,
         2 Ja 1965, p. 6.

         On Malcolm's attempt to bring the Afro-American
         problem to the U.N. Gives a detailed summary of the
         points in Malcolm's position. (400)

4A-92   "Negro Protest Supported by President." Times
         (London), 5 Feb 1965, p. 10.

         On the civil rights demonstrations in Selma.
         Briefly mentions Malcolm's appearance there. (500)

4A-93   "Speed Negro Vote, Judge Tells Alabama." New York
         Times, 5 Feb 1965, p. 17.

         In a lengthy article on civil rights demonstrations
         in Alabama, the reporter mentions Malcolm's speech to
         civil rights workers there. (60)

4A-94   "Malcolm X Barred from France." Times (London), 10
         Feb 1965, p. 11.

         Gives several quotes from Malcolm on his experience
         of being barred from entering France. (250)

4A-95   "Malcolm X Barred by French Security." <u>New York</u>
        <u>Times</u>, 10 Feb 1965, p. 3.

        Relays the account of Malcolm being denied entry
        into France. (150)

4A-96   "Malcolm X Off to Smethwick." <u>Times</u> (London), 12 Feb
        1965, p. 7.

        Report of a speech delivered in England. Reporter
        notes the audience response and gives several quotes
        from Malcolm on the racial problems in England. (800)

4A-97   "Malcolm X's Views Deplored." <u>Times</u> (London), 13 Feb
        1965, p. 6.

        Report on Malcolm's activities in England.
        Includes the responses of several local politicians.
        (250)

4A-98   "Aid to Malcolm X Assailed by BBC." <u>New York Times</u>,
        14 Feb 1965, p. 24.

        Reports criticism by officials of the English
        government for the BBC's role in escorting Malcolm
        around England. (25).

4A-99   "Malcolm X Returns." <u>New York Times</u>, 14 Feb 1965, p.
        24.

        News item announcing Malcolm's return to the U.S.
        (25)

4A-100 "Bomb Thrown into Malcolm X House." <u>Times</u> (London),
        15 Feb 1965, p. 8.

        News item on the firebombing of Malcolm's home.
        (150)

4A-101 "Malcolm X Flees Firebomb Attack." <u>New York Times</u>, 15
        Feb 1965, p. 1.

Account of the firebombing of Malcolm's house.
Mentions Malcolm's suspicions that it was the work of
Black Muslims or the Ku Klux Klan. (450)

4A-102 "Malcolm Accuses Muslims of Blaze; They Point to
        Him." New York Times, 16 Feb 1965, p. 18.

Report of a speech Malcolm delivered in Harlem in
which he blames the Nation of Islam for bombing his
house. He repeats assertions of meetings between
Nazis and Nation of Islam. Article notes the Muslims'
response that Malcolm bombed his own house for the
publicity. (300)

4A-103 "Bottle of Gasoline Found on a Dresser in Malcolm X
        Home." New York Times, 17 Feb 1965, p. 34.

Report of a bottle of gasoline found in Malcolm's
house by investigators of the bombing. Malcolm denies
knowledge of how it got there. (300)

4A-104 "Malcolm X." Times (London), 19 Feb 1965, p. 17.

News item on a parliamentary official who asked
that Malcolm be designated an undesirable alien and
refused further admittance to England. (100)

4A-105 "Malcolm X Averts Writ by Moving Out." New York
        Times, 19 Feb 1965, p. 31.

Reports Malcolm's move from his house in order to
avoid eviction based on a suit filed by the Nation of
Islam, holder of the title to the house. (100)

4A-106 "Malcolm Shot Dead at Harlem Rally." Times (London),
        22 Feb 1965, p. 10.

Report of the assassination. Gives details and
speculates on the involvement of the Nation of
Islam. Mentions attacks Malcolm had made on the
Nation of Islam regarding their contacts with the Ku
Klux Klan. (700)

4A-107 "Malcolm X Shot to Death at Rally Here." New York
       Times, 22 Feb 1965, p. 1.

       Picture of Malcolm being carried from the Audubon
       Ballroom.

4A-108 "Malcolm Knew He Was a Marked Man." New York Times,
       22 Feb 1965, p. 1.

       Report of an interview that took place four days
       before the assassination in which Malcolm predicts he
       would be killed by members of the Nation of Islam and
       lists the reasons why they want him dead. (550)

4A-109 "Three Other Negroes Wounded--One Is Held in
       Killing." New York Times, 22 Feb 1965, p. 1.

       Detailed account of the assassination. Includes
       statements from eyewitnesses. (2000)

4A-110 "Police Save Suspect from Crowd." New York Times, 22
       Feb 1965, p. 10.

       On the immediate aftermath of the assassination.
       Centers on police descriptions of their rescue of
       Thomas Hagan [Talmadge Hayer], one of Malcolm's
       alleged assassins. (600)

4A-111 "Malcolm X Lived in Two Worlds, White and Black, Both
       Bitter." New York Times, 22 Feb 1965, p. 10.

       Summary of Malcolm X's life up to and including the
       split with Elijah Muhammad. (800)

4A-112 "Other Muslims Fear for Lives." New York Times, 22
       Feb 1965, p. 10.

       Details various assaults on ex-Muslims around the
       country, focusing on Leon Ameer, a chief aide to
       Malcolm. (500)

4A-113 "Harlem Is Quiet as News Spreads." New York Times, 22
       Feb 1965, p. 11.

Impressions of the atmosphere in Harlem following the assassination. Reporter's summary is that many of Malcolm's followers are still in shock but rumors of revenge circulate. (500)

4A-114 "Malcolm Asked Gun Permit after Home Was Bombed." New York Times, 22 Feb 1965, p. 10.

Report of Malcolm's application for a permit to carry a pistol. Includes his remark that he would carry one whether or not the permit was approved. (150)

4A-115 "Clay's Apartment in Chicago Is Burned by a Suspicious Fire." New York Times, 22 Feb 1965, p. 10.

Report of arson at Clay's Chicago home. Occurred seven hours after Malcolm's assassination. (150)

4A-116 "Precautions Taken." New York Times, 22 Feb 1965, p. 10.

Details attempts to protect Elijah Muhammad, including police surveillance of his home and surveillance at O'Hare Airport to intercept any of Malcolm's followers. (125)

4A-117 "Nationalist Group Left Leaderless by Murder." New York Times, 22 Feb 1965, p. 10.

Short report on the state of the OAAU. (75)

4A-118 "Malcolm Fought for Top Power in Muslim Movement, and Lost." New York Times, 22 Feb 1965, p. 11.

Summary of the power struggle within the Nation of Islam that led to Malcolm's resignation. Includes a history of the Nation of Islam and previous power struggles involving Elijah Muhammad in the 1930s. (600)

4A-119 "Rights Leaders Decry Violence." New York Times, 22
       Feb 1965, p. 11.

       Comments from several civil rights leaders,
       including James Foreman, Dr. King, and Julian Bond,
       expressing shock at the assassination. (500)

4A-120 "Malcolm X's Sister Says He Was Living in Fear." New
       York Times, 22 Feb 1965, p. 11.

       Short report about Malcolm's sister, Ella Collins,
       on his suspicions of an attempt on his life. (60)

4A-121 "Muhammad Says Muslims Played No Part in Slaying."
       New York Times, 23 Feb 1965, p. 1.

       Report of a press conference by Elijah Muhammad
       where he states that he had no prior knowledge of
       Malcolm's assassination. Includes a survey of
       precautionary measures taken by police to prevent
       further violence. (500)

4A-122 "Muslim Mosque Burns in Harlem." New York Times, 23
       Feb 1965, p. 1.

       Report on the burning of the Nation of Islam's
       Mosque in Harlem. Includes summary on the progress of
       the police investigation and funeral plans for
       Malcolm. (2000)

4A-123 "Special Phone Set Up for Facts on Slaying." New York
       Times, 23 Feb 1965, p. 20.

       Note on the police attempt to gather information on
       the assassination. (75)

4A-124 "Malcolm X Led Clay to Muslims." New York Times, 23
       Feb 1965, p. 21.

       Recounting of the relationship between Malcolm and
       Clay. Points out the role Malcolm played in
       recruiting Clay to the Nation of Islam. (250)

4A-125 "Heavy Police Guard for Black Muslim Mosque." _Times_
       (London), 23 Feb 1965, p. 10.

       Details of the aftermath of the assassination.
       Details previous confrontations between the followers
       of Malcolm and Muhammad. (600)

4A-126 "Set Back to Cause of Progress." _Times_ (London), 23
       Feb 1965, p. 10.

       Report of a statement made by James Baldwin on the
       assassination. (150)

4A-127 "After Malcolm X." _Times_ (London), 23 Feb 1965, p.
       13.

       Editorial on Malcolm's death. Sees it as marking
       the beginning of a decline in militant nationalism
       among Afro-Americans. (350)

4A-128 "Mosque Fire Stirs Fear of Vendetta in Malcolm
       Case." _New York Times_, 24 Feb 1965, p. 1.

       Listing of police precautions to halt possible
       violence. Includes stories of threats against Nation
       of Islam businesses, Elijah Muhammad, and the funeral
       home holding Malcolm's body. (1000)

4A-129 "Peking Urges Violent Reply." _New York Times_, 24 Feb
       1965, p. 30.

       Report of a radio broadcast from Peking which urges
       a reply of 'revolutionary violence' to Malcolm X's
       assassination. (50)

4A-130 "A Racist Crime, Cubans Say." _New York Times_, 24 Feb
       1965, p. 30.

       Report of a Cuban newspaper that viewed Malcolm's
       assassination as an attempt to halt the struggle
       against racial discrimination. (25)

4A-131 "CORE Chief Calls Slaying Political." New York Times,
       24 Feb 1965, p. 30.

       Statement from James Farmer implying that there was
       international intrigue behind Malcolm's assassination.
       (300)

4A-132 "Cassius Clay Says He Is Not 'Scared' of Killing
       Reprisal." New York Times, 24 Feb 1965, p. 31.

       Clay's reaction to death threats against him in the
       wake of Malcolm's assassination. (75)

4A-133 "Muslims Enraged by 'Sneak Attack.'" New York Times,
       24 Feb 1965, p. 31.

       Describes Nation of Islam reaction to the burning
       of their Mosque. (300)

4A-134 "Black Muslim Mosque Is Burnt." Times (London), 24
       Feb 1965, p. 11.

       Report of Mosque burnings in New York and San
       Francisco. (350)

4A-135 "Hunt for Killers in Malcolm Case 'On Right Track.'"
       New York Times, 25 Feb 1965, p. 1.

       Update on police investigation and an analysis of
       the effect of Malcolm X's departure from the Nation of
       Islam. Also a description of visitors to view Malcolm
       X's body. (600)

4A-136 "Closing of 125th St. Stores to Honor Malcolm X
       Asked." New York Times, 25 Feb 1965, p. 18.

       Story on a demand made by the Federation for
       Independent Political Action (FIPA), a Harlem-based
       group. (50)

4A-137 "China Reds Say Malcolm X Was Slain by 'Imperial-
       ists.'" New York Times, 25 Feb 1965, p. 18.

Report on an editorial in a Peking newspaper. (100)

4A-138 "Stores Prodded to Hail Malcolm." New York Times, 26
Feb 1965, p. 1.

Story on Jesse Gray and the FIPA's attempt to close
stores in remembrance of Malcolm. Further reports on
threats by and against the Nation of Islam, and a
short report on a memorial service in Detroit. (600)

4A-139 "Malcolm Called a Martyr Abroad." New York Times, 26
Feb 1965, p. 15.

Report on a speech by Carl Rowan in which he states
that Malcolm's ideas had been misunderstood abroad and
that was why he was being hailed as a hero. (250)

4A-140 "Black Muslim Guard Held in Murder of Malcolm X." New
York Times, 27 Feb 1965, p. 1.

Reports the first arrest in Malcolm's assassination. Includes story on the FIPA attempt to have
stores close in Harlem. (500)

4A-141 "Muhammad Says Muslims Must Protect Themselves." New
York Times, 27 Feb 1965, p. 1.

Report on the annual convention of the Nation of
Islam. Lengthy quotes from Elijah Muhammad on
Malcolm's death. (700)

4A-142 "Without Malcolm X." Economist, 27 Feb 1965, p. 888.

Story on Malcolm's assassination. Lists reasons
why the Nation of Islam could be involved. Includes
thoughts on Malcolm's potential impact on radicalizing
Afro-Americans in the North. (800)

4A-143 "Assassination of Malcolm X." Illustrated London
News, 27 Feb 1965, p. 4.

Short story on Malcolm's assassination and the aftermath. (250)

4A-144 "Death of Malcolm X." New York Times, 27 Feb 1965, p. 24.

Letter to the editor critical of a NYT editorial. Calls Malcolm a 'truthful and sincere man.' (150)

4A-145 "Black Muslim on Murder Charge." Times (London), 27 Feb 1965, p. 8.

News item on the arrest of a Muslim in Malcolm's murder. (200)

4A-146 "Harlem Is Quiet as Crowds Watch Malcolm X Rites." New York Times, 28 Feb 1965, p. 1.

Report on Malcolm's funeral. Lists organizations represented and includes some excerpts from the oration. (1000)

4A-147 "Harlem Stores Have a Slow Day." New York Times, 28 Feb 1965, p. 72.

Story on business activity on the day of Malcolm's funeral. (200)

4A-148 "Malcolm Buried as True Muslim Despite the Unorthodox Ritual." New York Times, 28 Feb 1965, p. 72.

Comparison of orthodox Islamic funerals with Malcolm's funeral. (500)

4A-149 "World Pays Little Attention to Malcolm Slaying." New York Times, 28 Feb 1965, p. 74.

Summary of NYT's foreign correspondents' reports on the impact of Malcolm's assassination. They found some concern in the Middle East, Africa, and the Caribbean, but little notice in Europe. (600)

4A-150 "Indonesians Invade U.S. Envoy's Home." New York
       Times, 1 Mar 1965, p. 4.

       Five hundred students invade, protesting Malcolm's
       assassination and the U.S. involvement in the Vietnam
       War. (500)

4A-151 "Malcolm X Termed Stimulus to Action." New York
       Times, 1 Mar 1965, p. 17.

       Afro-American leaders, Bayard Rustin and Constance
       Baker Motley, quoted as saying that people should use
       Malcolm's death to focus more attention on the
       struggle against racism. (150)

4A-152 "Voice of Malcolm X." New York Times, 1 Mar 1965, p.
       26.

       Letter to the editor disagreeing with an editorial
       on Malcolm. Author calls Malcolm a leader of courage
       and foresight. (300)

4A-153 "Man Held in Black Muslim Scuffle." Times (London), 1
       Mar 1965, p. 10.

       Report on a fight at the Nation of Islam annual
       convention in Chicago, and a short note on Malcolm's
       funeral. (200)

4A-154 "Widow of Malcolm X Speaks with Police about His
       Slaying." New York Times, 2 Mar 1965, p. 19.

       Report on a meeting between police and Malcolm's
       widow. Article also describes various fund appeals to
       assist the widow and her children. (400)

4A-155 "Two Malcolm Men Seized in Bronx." New York Times, 3
       Mar 1965, p. 53.

       Report of a police raid on the home of one of
       Malcolm's assistants. Officers found weapons.
       Includes a note on growing Muslim rivalry. (500)

4A-156 "Third Man Seized in Malcolm Case." New York Times, 4
       Mar 1965, p. 14.

       Report noting the arrest of Thomas Johnson, third
       suspect in the slaying of Malcolm. (250)

4A-157 "Malcolm X-ism Feared by Rustin." New York Times, 4
       Mar 1965, p. 15.

       Report of a speech by Bayard Rustin in which he
       blames violence on social conditions. He also
       recounts a meeting between Malcolm and Coretta Scott
       King where Malcolm stated that he was drifting from
       his former racial views. (300)

4A-158 "Malcolm Called Needed and Responsible Leader." New
       York Times, 5 Mar 1965, p. 32.

       Letter to the editor by a white minister who
       asserts that Malcolm spoke for a larger number of
       Afro-Americans. (300)

4A-159 "Freedom Denied to Black Muslim." New York Times, 5
       Mar 1965, p. 68.

       Norman Butler, accused assassin of Malcolm, is
       denied release on Habeas Corpus. Article details
       Butler's criminal background. (500)

4A-160 "Death and Transfiguration." Time, 5 Mar 1965, p. 23.

       Report on the assassination. Reporter calls
       Malcolm a 'disaster' for the civil rights movement.
       Mentions that Malcolm is being hailed as a hero by
       many. (500)

4A-161 "Wives of Suspects Testify in Slaying." New York
       Times, 5 Mar 1965, p. 10.

       Report on the testimony of Johnson's and Butler's
       wives, relating that they were at home during the
       assassination. (150)

4A-162 "Tragedy of Malcolm X." America, 6 Mar 1965, p. 303.

        Editorial on the 'wasted' life and tragedy of
        Malcolm. (200)

4A-163 "Malcolm X." Nation, 8 Mar 1965, p. 239.

        Editorial on Malcolm's assassination. Views
        Malcolm as a separatist and argues for more rapid
        change in order to disprove the 'Malcolm X's'. (350)

4A-164 "Death of a Desparado." Newsweek, 8 Mar 1965, p. 24.

        Story giving detailed account of Malcolm's
        assassination and a review of his life. Includes
        comments on his changing racial attitudes. (1000)

4A-165 "Now It's Negroes vs. Negroes in America's Racial
        Violence." U.S. News and World Report, 8 Mar 1965,
        p. 7.

        Report on Malcolm's assassination and the
        aftermath. Includes brief comments by Dr. King, Carl
        Rowan, and mentions African press coverage of the
        assassination. (600)

4A-166 "Jury Hears Malcolm's Widow." New York Times, 10 Mar
        1965, p. 8.

        Short note that Malcolm's wife testified for 20
        minutes at the trial of his accused assassins. (50)

4A-167 "Four Are Indicted Here in Malcolm X Case." New York
        Times, 11 Mar 1965, p. 66.

        Reports the indictments of Hayer, Butler, and
        Johnson in Malcolm's assassination, and the indictment
        of Reuben Francis, Malcolm X's bodyguard, for shooting
        Hayer. (150)

4A-168 "Vendetta by Rivals Feared." Senior Scholastic, 11
        Mar 1965, p. 21.

Comment on the possibilities of Muslim rivalry
ending in more violence. (300)

4A-169 "Malcolm X Aide Dead in Boston." New York Times, 14
      Mar 1965, p. 57.

Death of Leon Ameer, an aide to Malcolm, under
mysterious circumstances. Details Ameer's life and
his association with Malcolm. (700)

4A-170 "Malcolm's Sister Takes Over: Says She Fears New
      Violence." New York Times, 16 Mar 1965, p. 33.

Press conference with Malcolm's sister, Ella
Collins, reporting her leadership of the OAAU. Brief
biographical background of Collins and reports her
plans for the organization. (500)

4A-171 "Lewiston Police Force Tripled after Report of Danger
      to Clay." New York Times, 21 Mar 1965, p. 24.

Report of death threats to Clay. (100)

4A-172 "Peking and Malcolm X." New Republic, 27 Mar 1965, p.
      8.

Editorial on the Chinese government's reaction to
Malcolm's assassination, a statement which lays the
blame on U.S. imperialism. Includes a poem written
for Malcolm which appeared in the Peoples Daily. (150)

4A-173 "Peking and Malcom X--A Reply." New Republic, 17 Apr
      1965, p. 44.

Letter to the editor in reply to a New Republic
editorial on Malcolm X. Reasserts the position that
Malcolm was the victim of U.S. imperialism. (400)

4A-174 "Malcolm's Widow Aided by Benefit." New York Times, 9
      Aug 1965, p. 28.

Report of a benefit performed by artists, including Dizzy Gillespie, Max Roach, and Leroi Jones, held to provide for the financial security of Malcolm's widow and children. (250)

4A-175 "Malcolm's a Harlem Idol on Eve of Murder Trial." New York Times, 6 Dec 1965, p. 46.

Assessment of Malcolm's impact. Finds Malcolm a dominant influence on Northern intellectual ghetto life. Includes interviews with his widow and Dr. Lewis Michaux. (500)

4A-176 "Malcolm X Murder Trial On." New York Times, 7 Dec 1965, p. 56.

Notes beginning of the trial of Hayer, Butler, and Johnson. (25)

4A-177 "Transit Strike Halts Malcolm X Case." New York Times, 5 Ja 1966, p. 16.

Note that a transit strike prohibited many jurors from reaching the courtroom. (50)

4A-178 "Selection of Jury Starts in Malcolm X Murder Case." New York Times, 13 Ja 1966, p. 13.

Notes selection of jury in the trial. Lists the names and addresses of jurors. (100)

4A-179 "Jury Selection is Lagging in Malcolm X Murder Case." New York Times, 14 Ja 1966, p. 18.

Note on problems of selecting jurors agreeable to the prosecution and the defense. (100)

4A-180 "Three More Jurors Are Chosen in Malcolm X Murder Trial." New York Times, 15 Ja 1966, p. 25.

Lists addresses, names, and occupations of three jurors selected in the trial. (125)

4A-181 "Three Malcolm X Jurors Chosen." New York Times, 19
        Ja 1966, p. 83.

        (25)

4A-182 "Jury Selection Completed in Malcolm X Murder." New
        York Times, 20 Ja 1966, p. 19.

        Lists names and occupations of jurors selected.
        (100)

4A-183 "Witness Recalls Malcolm Killing." New York Times, 22
        Ja 1966, p. 30.

        Reports testimony of a follower of Malcolm, Carey
        Thomas, who saw the three accused shoot Malcolm.
        Article includes a summary of the prosecution's
        opening statement. (400)

4A-184 "Defense Still Tries to Shake Witness of Malcolm
        Killing." New York Times, 22 Ja 1966, p. 21.

        Reports the cross-examination of witness Carey
        Thomas. (100)

4A-185 "Malcolm X Guard Explains Inaction." New York Times,
        27 Ja 1966, p. 37.

        Carey Thomas, follower and bodyguard of Malcolm,
        explains he did not shoot at the assassins for fear of
        hitting bystanders. (150)

4A-186 "Witnesses Point to Two in Malcolm Slaying." New York
        Times, 1 Feb 1966, p. 22.

        Additional witnesses, another bodyguard, and one
        bystander, point out the defendants as the ones who
        shot Malcolm. (200)

4A-187 "Malcolm Witness Heard in Secret." New York Times, 4
        Feb 1966, p. 38.

Reports a secret witness, who feared for his life, who saw the assassination and implicated the defendants. Article describes the defense strategy which is to prove that Malcolm was the victim of a conspiracy within his own organization. (400)

4A-188 "Policeman Is Heard at Malcolm X Trial." New York Times, 5 Feb 1966, p. 17.

Police officer testifies how he rescued one of the defendants, Hayer, from the crowd after Malcolm's assassination. (100)

4A-189 "Guard Admits Lie Over Malcolm X." New York Times, 9 Feb 1966, p. 50.

A bodyguard, Charles Blackwell, admits he lied to protect himself from being called a coward. (200)

4A-190 "Malcolm X Witness Recaptured Here." New York Times, 10 Feb 1966, p. 41.

Reuben Frances, a Malcolm bodyguard, was recaptured after jumping bail. Was accused of shooting one of the defendants, Hayer, at the scene of the assassination. (150)

4A-191 "Print Found in Bomb, Malcolm Jury Told." New York Times, 11 Feb 1966, p. 21.

Testimony that one of the defendants left a fingerprint on a smoke bomb detonated at the assassination site to distract attention. (100)

4A-192 "Thumbprint Linked to Malcolm Trial." New York Times, 12 Feb 1966, p. 12.

Report of a thumbprint on a smoke bomb. Print belonged to defendant Hayer. (125)

4A-193 "Daily Drama of Malcolm X Trial Is Nearing End." New York Times, 14 Feb 1966, p. 22.

Portrait of the courtroom describing the
prosecution and defense lawyers. (400)

4A-194 "Malcolm X's Widow Scores Suspects." New York Times,
       18 Feb 1966, p. 66.

       Quotes from Betty Shabazz, Malcolm's widow,
       testimony. Article mentions memorial march to be held
       sponsored by the NAACP and other groups. (400)

4A-195 "Prosecution Rests in Malcolm X Case." New York
       Times, 19 Feb 1966, p. 21.

       Describes testimony of a reporter who was at the
       assassination scene and identified Hayer as having
       shot Malcolm. (150)

4A-196 "Seventy-Five March to Mark Malcolm's Death." New
       York Times, 21 Feb 1966, p. 45.

       Description of memorial march organized by the
       NAACP, the Urban League, CORE, and other groups. (150)

4A-197 "Defense Is Opened in Malcolm Case." New York Times,
       22 Feb 1966, p. 16.

       A review of the defense strategy which is to prove
       that two of the defendants, Butler and Johnson, were
       not present at the assassination and that Hayer was an
       innocent bystander. (300)

4A-198 "Defendant Denies Shooting Malcolm." New York Times,
       24 Feb 1966, p. 27.

       Hayer denies shooting Malcolm but can't explain how
       his thumbprint got on the smoke bomb.

4A-199 "Defendant Admits Killing Malcolm X." New York Times,
       1 Mar 1966, p. 1.

       Hayer admits killing Malcolm but denies Butler and
       Johnson were involved. States that three other people

assisted him. Contends he was offered money to kill Malcolm. (400)

4A-200 "Malcolm X Case Confession." _Times_ (London), 1 Mar 1966, p. 12.

Report of Hayer's confession. (80)

4A-201 "Malcolm Witness Claims Innocence." _New York Times_, 2 Mar 1966, p. 50.

Defendant Butler denies he was at the scene of the assassination. Details his whereabouts. (250)

4A-202 "An Order to Kill Malcolm Hinted." _New York Times_, 3 Mar 1966, p. 24.

Prosecution notes the presence of John Ali, a top Nation of Islam official, in New York on the day of Malcolm's assassination. (300)

4A-203 "Jury Hears an Alibi in Malcolm Murder." _New York Times_, 4 Mar 1966, p. 16.

Defendant Johnson states that he was at home on the day of Malcolm's assassination. (100)

4A-204 "Testimony Is Ended in Malcolm X Case." _New York Times_, 5 Mar 1966, p. 10.

Short note marking the end of testimony at the trial. (100)

4A-205 "Defense Sums Up in Malcolm Case." _New York Times_, 8 Mar 1966, p. 24.

Restatement of the defense's position. (300)

4A-206 "Malcolm Slaying Called a 'Lesson.'" _New York Times_, 11 Mar 1966, p. 84.

Restatement of the prosecution's case. (400)

4A-207 "Malcolm Jury Finds Three Guilty." New York Times, 11
       Mar 1966, p. 1.

       Review of the trial in the aftermath of the guilty
       verdict. (1000)

4A-208 "Malcolm X Case Convictions." Times (London), 12 Mar
       1966, p. 8.

       Report of trial outcome. (50)

4A-209 "Who Issued the Orders." Newsweek, 21 Mar 1966, p.
       36.

       Article on the outcome of the murder trial of
       Malcolm's assassins. Points out that the trial did
       not solve the question of who was responsible. (350)

4A-210 "Three Get Life Terms in Malcolm Case." New York
       Times, 15 Apr 1966, p. 36.

       Describes the courtroom scene at sentencing. (300)

4A-211 "Negroes Sentenced in Malcolm X Case." Times
       (London), 16 Apr 1966, p. 8.

       (50)

4A-212 "Mourners Mark Malcolm X Day." New York Times, 20 May
       1966, p. 34.

       Descriptions of several ceremonies held in honor of
       Malcolm. Includes quotes from Ella Collins on her
       plan to rebuild the OAAU. (400)

4A-213 "Whitney Young Urges Attempt Be Made to Reach Ghetto
       Unreachables." New York Times, 1 Aug 1966, p. 14.

       Report on Young's speech at the National Urban

League Convention. Several groups picketed the
convention, including the W.E.B. DuBois Clubs and a
group calling themselves followers of Malcolm X. They
accused the Urban League of being Uncle Toms. (500)

4A-214 "United Front for Black Power Urged at Rally Here."
        New York Times, 15 Aug 1966, p. 18.

        Story of a Harlem rally sponsored by CORE.
        Speakers referred to the legacy of Malcolm X several
        times. (400)

4A-215 "Malcolm X." New York Times, 17 Aug 1966, p. 38.

        Letter to the editor responding to a New York Times
        article that compared Stokely Carmichael to Malcolm
        X. Writer points out that Malcolm had retracted his
        anti-white beliefs but Carmichael has not. (150)

4A-216 "Williams to Handle Three Muslims' Appeal in Malcolm
        Killing; Black Muslims Deny Role in Killing and
        Trial." New York Times, 8 Sept 1966, p. 33.

        Story describing Edward Bennett Williams' plans to
        appeal sentences of the convicted assassins. Story
        speculates that the Nation of Islam is paying the
        legal expenses for the case. (150)

4A-217 "March in Harlem Honors Malcolm." New York Times, 23
        Feb 1967, p. 26.

        Story of a black nationalist march in honor of
        Malcolm X. Crowd was addressed by Ella Collins and
        Stokely Carmichael. (250)

4A-218 "Baldwin's Dress Rehearsal on Play on Malcolm X."
        Times (London), 25 Nov 1967, p. 8.

        Report on James Baldwin's presence in London to
        work on a play about Malcolm X. Play is scheduled to
        open on Broadway in 1968. (150)

4A-219 "Beautification of Malcolm X." <u>Time</u>, 1 Mar 1968, p. 16.
    Article about several observances held across the country to honor Malcolm. (500)

4A-220 "St. Malcolm X." <u>Newsweek</u>, 3 Mar 1969, p. 27.

    Story on the canonization of Malcolm, four years after his death. Points out how the rapid evolution of Malcolm's thought in his last year has allowed a disparate group of people to claim his legacy. (400)

4A-221 "Historical Primer." <u>Time</u> 12 June 1972, p. 62.

    Brief review of a Warner Brothers documentary on Malcolm's life. (250)

4A-222 "Who Killed Malcolm?" <u>Newsweek</u>, 7 May 1979, p. 39.

    Story of Hayer, convicted assassin of Malcolm. He now admits his guilt and says he was part of a Nation of Islam hit squad. Hayer still maintains the innocence of Butler and Johnson. (600)

4A-223 "Killer of Malcolm X Approved for Parole by New York Board." <u>New York Times</u>, 8 May 1985, p. 16.

    Article noting that Norman Butler, now called Abdul Aziz, is to be released on parole on June 24, 1985. (400)

IVB   NEWS REPORTS--AFRO-AMERICAN PRESS

4B-1   "Mr. Malcolm X at New York Temple Sunday."   Amsterdam
       News, 5 Ja 1957, p. 3.

       Item announcing a series of public lectures by
       Malcolm. (200)

4B-2   "The Muhammads, What Are They?"   Amsterdam News, 6 Apr
       1957, p. 4.

       Interview with Malcolm. He answers basic questions
       about the beliefs of the Nation of Islam, including
       their positions on integration, baptism, and diet.
       (500)

4B-3   "Mr. X Tells What Islam Means."   Amsterdam News, 20
       Apr 1957, p. 4.

       Outlines the basic beliefs and historical back-
       ground of the Nation of Islam. Malcolm comments on
       his past life of crime and drug addiction. (400)

4B-4   "God's Angry Men."   Amsterdam News, 27 Apr 1957, p. 18.

       Article by Malcolm on the religious beliefs of the
       Nation of Islam. (1000)

4B-5   "God's Angry Men Tangle with Police."   Amsterdam News,
       4 May 1957, p. 18.

       On a confrontation between police and a Muslim.
       Explains Malcolm's role, as the leader of the New York
       Muslims, demanding information on the condition of the
       injured Muslim. (2000)

4B-6   "God's Angry Men." Amsterdam News, 4 May 1957, p. 6.

        Article by Malcolm in which he discusses the role
of slavery in the mental bondage of Afro-Americans.
(1000)

4B-7   "Say Police Take Movies of Muslims." Amsterdam News,
        11 May 1957, p. 1.

        Charge by Malcolm that police have been harassing
the Nation of Islam at its mosque in Harlem. (400)

4B-8   "Menace to Race." Amsterdam News, 11 May 1957, p. 8.

        Letter to the editor suggesting that Malcolm be
given a regular column in the Amsterdam News so that
he could enlighten those people who are a "menace to
the race." (125)

4B-9   "God's Angry Men." Amsterdam News, 18 May 1957, p. 5.

        Article by Malcolm in which he continues his dis-
cussion of the psychological effects of slavery.
(1000)

4B-10   "God's Angry Men." Amsterdam News, 25 May 1957, p. 9.

        Beginning of the regular column by Malcolm. In
this article he discusses the religion of Islam and
contrasts it to Christianity. (750)

4B-11   "God's Angry Men." Amsterdam News, 1 June 1957, p.
        20.

        In this column, Malcolm criticizes Christianity as
having assured the continued enslavement of Afro-
Americans. (1000)

4B-12   "God's Angry Men." Amsterdam News, 8 June 1957, p. 6.

        Malcolm comments on Bible prophecy and on the
afterlife. (500)

4B-13   "Muslim Leader Malcolm X Speaks at Abyssinian
         Baptist." <u>Amsterdam News</u>, 15 June 1957, p. 25.

         Report of a speech that was part of a series
         entitled "Unity of Harlem's Black Citizens." Malcolm
         argues that only Islam can unify Afro-Americans. (400)

4B-14   "Likes Mr. X." <u>Amsterdam News</u>, 22 June 1957, p. 8.

         Letter to the editor expressing pleasure at
         Malcolm's columns. (50)

4B-15   "Moslem Speaker Electrifies Garvey Crowd." <u>Amsterdam
         News</u>, 10 Aug 1957, p. 4.

         On a speech by Malcolm. He attacks Afro-American
         leaders as being puppets for white people and praises
         the type of leadership represented by Marcus Garvey.
         (200)

4B-16   "Malcolm X in Detroit for Two Weeks." <u>Amsterdam News</u>,
         31 Aug 1957, p. 16.

         On a speech Malcolm delivered at the Detroit
         Mosque. In it he attacks Afro-American leaders and
         intellectuals for not doing enough to alter the social
         conditions in the Afro-American community. (400)

4B-17   "Malcolm X Making Hit in Detroit." <u>Amsterdam News</u>, 7
         Sept 1957, p. 16.

         Report on Malcolm's lectures in Detroit. He is
         quoted on the problem of police brutality in the Afro-
         American community. (300)

4B-18   "Malcolm X Returns; Detroit Muslims Grow." <u>Amsterdam
         News</u>, 26 Oct 1957, p. 3.

         On Malcolm's two-month Detroit visit. Reports that
         membership in the Detroit Mosque tripled. (250)

4B-19   "Malcolm X in Boston." Amsterdam News, 9 Nov 1957, p.
         17.

         On a visit to Boston to assist Louis X (Farrakhan)
         in building the membership of the Boston Mosque. (150)

4B-20   "Malcolm Shabazz Speaker at D.C. Brotherhood Feast."
         Amsterdam News, 30 Nov 1957, p. 4.

         Report on a speech sponsored by the D.C. Mosque.
         (100)

4B-21   "Malcolm X Speaks in Los Angeles." Amsterdam News, 7
         Dec 1957, p. 17.

         Report on a speech delivered in Los Angeles to a
         full house. (150)

4B-22   "Malcolm X Speaks in Detroit Again." Amsterdam News,
         14 Dec 1957, p. 7.

         Malcolm comments on the growth of Islam in the U.S.
         and on the unbiased role of the Afro-American media in
         its coverage of the Nation of Islam. (150)

4B-23   "700 Attend Muslim Program." Amsterdam News, 11 Ja
         1958, p. 14.

         Report of a Muslim rally in Harlem. Speakers
         included Malcolm and Louis X (Farrakhan). (300)

4B-24   "Malcolm Wed; It's a Surprise." Amsterdam News, 25 Ja
         1958, p. 4.

         Report on the marriage of Malcolm to Betty X. (150)

4B-25   "Christians Walk Out on Moslems." Amsterdam News, 26
         Apr 1958, p. 1.

         Several Christian ministers walk out of a speech by
         Malcolm in Los Angeles. (250)

4B-26 "Arab Director, Malcolm X, Hit U.S. Press, Radio,
       TV." Amsterdam News, 3 May 1958, p. 5.

       At a press conference in Los Angeles, Malcolm calls
       on Arabs to build alliances with Afro-Americans. (300)

4B-27 "Malcolm X at Howard as Speaker." Amsterdam News, 11
       Feb 1961, p. 30.

       Short news report of a speaking engagement by
       Malcolm X at Howard University. (150)

4B-28 "Muslims to Sue Adlai Stevenson." Amsterdam News, 25
       Feb 1961, p. 1.

       Report of a statement by Malcolm X that the Nation
       of Islam would sue Adlai Stevenson, U.S. Ambassador to
       the U.N., for falsely accusing the Muslims of starting
       a riot. Article goes on to mention several radical
       Afro-American groups that were involved in picketing
       at the U.N. (600)

4B-29 "Malcolm May, May Not Talk at Howard." Amsterdam
       News, 25 Feb 1961, p. 2.

       Report of an attempt by the Howard University
       student chapter of the NAACP to sponsor a lecture by
       Malcolm X. (280)

4B-30 "Harvard Hears Malcolm, NAACP Speaker." Amsterdam
       News, 8 Apr 1961, p. 4.

       Report of a debate between Malcolm and a represent-
       ative of the NAACP. In his speech Malcolm demands a
       separate state for Afro-Americans. (280)

4B-31 "Breaking Up a Meeting." Amsterdam News, 10 June
       1961, p. 13.

       Report of an NAACP rally that was disrupted by
       black nationalists. The writer reports that Malcolm X
       was in attendance but did not participate in the
       disruption. (800)

4B-32 "Separation or Death, Muslim Watchword." <u>Amsterdam
       News</u>, 1 July 1961, p. 1.

       Report of a Muslim rally in which Malcolm demanded
       the separation of the races. (500)

4B-33 "Muslim Charges Police Brutality." <u>Amsterdam News</u>, 19
       Aug 1961, p. 1.

       Report of a member of the Nation of Islam who was
       beaten by the police. Article quotes Malcolm on the
       peaceful nature of Muslims and on the Muslim belief in
       self-defense. (300)

4B-34 "Police Probe Plot to Kill Elijah Muhammad." <u>Amster-
       dam News</u>, 26 Aug 1961, p. 1.

       Report of a plot to kill Elijah Muhammad at an
       upcoming rally sponsored by the Nation of Islam.
       Article quotes Malcolm on the right to self-defense
       and on security precautions at the rally. (300)

4B-35 "College Heads Cancel Out Malcolm X Speech."
       <u>Amsterdam News</u>, 21 Oct 1961, p. 1.

       Short item on the ban on Malcolm from speaking at
       Queens College. (100)

4B-36 "Minister Malcolm X." <u>Muhammad Speaks</u>, Dec 1961, p.
       11.

       Short item mentioning Malcolm as eloquent and
       fiery. (50)

4B-37 "Malcolm X Speaks in New Rochelle." <u>Amsterdam News</u>, 9
       Dec 1961, p. 9.

       Short news item on a speech Malcolm delivered at a
       Baptist church. (200)

4B-38 "Negro Leadership Blasted." <u>Muhammad Speaks</u>, Ja 1962,
       p. 24.

Report of a speech by Malcolm at Howard University
in which he attacks the leadership of the civil rights
movement for its policy of integration and
nonviolence. (400)

4B-39   "Malcolm X at Community." Amsterdam News, 20 Ja 1962,
        p. 4.

Note of a debate between Malcolm and Bayard Rustin
on the topic, separation or integration. (50)

4B-40   "Muslims' Victory is Far-Reaching." Amsterdam News, 3
        Feb 1962, p. 1.

Article on a court decision granting Muslim prison
inmates the right to practice their religion. Quotes
from Malcolm on the decision. (300)

4B-41   "Three Hundred Switch to Muslims in Phoenix."
        Amsterdam News, 10 Feb 1962, p. 19.

Story of a mass conversion after a speech by Elijah
Muhammad. Malcolm comments on the difficulties the
Nation of Islam has had with Christian ministers.
(150)

4B-42   "Malcolm X, Rustin Debating." Muhammad Speaks, Mar
        1962, p. 7.

Note on a debate on the topic of integration or
separation. (100)

4B-43   "Malcolm X Speaks at Abyssinian." Amsterdam News, 14
        Apr 1962, p. 18.

Story of an upcoming speech by Malcolm as part of a
series entitled, "Which Way the Negro." Story
mentions that church leaders had tried to block
Malcolm's appearance. (200)

4B-44   "Two Thousand Hear Malcolm X Rap Powell." Amsterdam
        News, 28 Apr 1962, p. 1.

Speech in which Malcolm demands that Adam C.
Powell request an investigation into the lynching
of an Afro-American in the south. Malcolm praises
Powell as the only Afro-American politician that
will stand up to white people. (400)

4B-45 "Brother to Brother." Muhammad Speaks, May 1962, p.
        17.

Picture with caption suggesting unity between Arab
Muslims and the Nation of Islam. Picture shows
Malcolm with the director of New York's Islamic
Center. (50)

4B-46 "Cops Slay Muslim on Coast." Amsterdam News, 5 May
        1962, p. 1.

Story of an incident between the Los Angeles police
and the Nation of Islam. Mentions Malcolm flying to
California to investigate. (150)

4B-47 "Malcolm X Heads Rally Sunday." Amsterdam News, 26
        May 1962, p. 4.

Story of a rally sponsored by the Nation of Islam.
(101)

4B-48 "Muslims Rally July 21." Amsterdam News, 14 July
        1962, p. 9.

Story of a Muslim rally which several other Afro-
American leaders were invited to attend. Rally was to
discuss drugs, unemployment, and other social
problems.

4B-49 "White Woman Offered $$ to Muslims." Amsterdam News,
        14 July 1962, p. 9.

Story of a white woman who offered $11,000 to the
Muslims for them to kill white people. She was taken
to a mental hospital. (150)

4B-50   "Muhammad Cites Awakening of Black Race."   Muhammad
        Speaks, 15 July 1962, p. 3.

        Speech by Elijah Muhammad in which he praises
        Malcolm for his help in building the Nation of Islam.
        (500)

4B-51   "Muslims Will Hold Rally."   Amsterdam News, 21 July
        1962, p. 5.

        Story of a mass rally with Malcolm listed as the
        principal speaker. (50)

4B-52   "2,500 at Muslim Rally."   Amsterdam News, 28 July
        1962, p. 33.

        Story of the rally. Quotes from Malcolm on the
        necessity of cleaning up the Afro-American community.
        (250)

4B-53   "Rally for Hospital Workers."   Muhammad Speaks, 31
        July 1962, p. 17.

        Picture of Malcolm addressing a community rally in
        Harlem. Also on the platform is A. Philip Randolph.
        (25)

4B-54   "Muslims Back Drive on Dope Racket; Support Fight of
        Hospital Workers."   Muhammad Speaks, 31 July 1962,
        p. 24.

        Picture of Malcolm speaking at an anti-drug rally
        in Harlem. Story on his speech at a community rally
        in support of hospital workers. In speech he calls
        for a united front of all Afro-American organizations.
        (250)

4B-55   "Malcolm Won't Be in Englewood."   Amsterdam News, 11
        Aug 1962, p. 1.

        Story on Malcolm's declining to speak to a New
        Jersey rally to protest segregation. (75)

4B-56   "Jackie, African Nationalist, in War, Peace Match."
        Muhammad Speaks, 15 Aug 1962, p. 2.

        Picture and story of Malcolm's attempt to mediate a
        dispute between Jackie Robinson and Louis Michaux over
        the hiring practices of a store in Harlem. (150)

4B-57   "Muslims Say: 'Welcome' to Probe." Amsterdam News, 25
        Aug 1962, p. 1.

        Story on a possible HUAC investigation of the
        Nation of Islam. Malcolm's response is that they
        should investigate white racist groups, not religious
        organizations. (200)

4B-58   "At Home and Abroad." Muhammad Speaks, 15 Sept 1962,
        p. 10.

        Editorial taken from a speech by Malcolm. Condemns
        the violence of the U.S. government while defending
        self-defense by Afro-Americans. (500)

4B-59   "Muslim Minister Rips Token Integration." Muhammad
        Speaks, 15 Sept 1962, p. 14.

        Article by Malcolm. States the futility of
        integration and demands a separate state. (700)

4B-60   "Malcolm X in Court." Amsterdam News, 17 Nov 1962, p.
        1.

        Story of a court appearance in Buffalo at the trial
        of several Muslims. Extensive quotes from Malcolm's
        testimony on Muslim beliefs and how they view the
        present Afro-American leadership. (600)

4B-61   "Muslims L.A. Trial Is Set." Amsterdam News, 8 Dec
        1962, p. 1.

        Story on the trial in L.A. Quotes from Malcolm on
        the unfairness of the press coverage. (150)

4B-62   "Muslim Minister Blasts Press Bias."   Muhammad Speaks,
        30 Dec 1962, p. 3.

        Statement by Malcolm on the bias of the press
        attending a trial involving an incident between the
        L.A. police and members of the Nation of Islam. (400)

4B-63   "Muslims Are 'Saturday Evening Post' Topic."
        Amsterdam News, 26 Ja 1963, p. 2.

        Story of an article which relates a scene where
        Malcolm dispersed a potentially violent crowd. (150)

4B-64   "Minister Malcolm X Addresses Mass Harlem Rally."
        Muhammad Speaks, 31 Ja 1963, p. 11.

        Picture of Malcolm addressing a rally of Afro-
        American and Latino hospital workers. (30)

4B-65   "New York Mosque Hosts 'Night with the FOI.'"
        Muhammad Speaks, 31 Ja 1963, p. 24.

        A Muslim-sponsored dinner where Malcolm was the
        keynote speaker. (150)

4B-66   "Justice Mocked at Muslim Trial in New York City."
        Muhammad Speaks, 4 Feb 1963, p. 4.

        Story of a demonstration against police brutality.
        (600)

4B-67   "Society and Malcolm X."   Amsterdam News, 9 Feb 1963,
        p. 9.

        Column by Gertrude Wilson in which she comments on
        how people are listening to Malcolm, but regrets the
        racial hatred of the Nation of Islam. (250)

4B-68   "Muslims Call U.S. 'A Police State.'"   Amsterdam News,
        23 Feb 1963, p. 1.

Speech by Malcolm at a Muslim rally in which he accuses the police of brutality. (300)

4B-69 "Keynote Speaker Blasts Parsons." Muhammad Speaks, 18 Mar 1963, p. 3.

Muslim convention keynoted by Malcolm. He attacks Judge Parsons, who had criticized the Nation of Islam for its racial attitudes. (600)

4B-70 "Rochester Negroes Unite for Freedom." Muhammad Speaks, 18 Mar 1963, p. 11.

Demonstration in which Malcolm spoke against police brutality. (400)

4B-71 "Ossie Davis and Ruby Dee Introduced by Minister Malcolm X." Muhammad Speaks, 1 Apr 1963, p. 21.

Picture of Malcolm introducing Davis and Dee at a fund raiser for the Nation of Islam. (25)

4B-72 "Powell Says 'Our Freedom Can't Wait.'" Muhammad Speaks, 15 Apr 1963, p. 1.

Story of a rally addressed by Adam C. Powell, Malcolm, and other Afro-American leaders. (500)

4B-73 "Malcolm X in Eyes of Nation." Amsterdam News, 27 Apr 1963, p. 1.

Story of a New York Times article on the Nation of Islam. Quotes the paper's perspective on Malcolm. (400)

4B-74 "A White Christian Answers the Muslims." Amsterdam News, 1 June 1963, p. 10.

Column by a priest who attacks the Nation of Islam and Malcolm for their belief in racial separation. (500)

4B-75   "Minister Blasts Mayor." Muhammad Speaks, 7 June
        1963, p. 1.

        Text of a telegram Malcolm sent to Mayor Samuel
        Yorty of Los Angeles criticizing the L.A. police for
        racism and brutality. (400)

4B-76   "Malcolm at Dem Club." Amsterdam News, 22 June 1963,
        p. 4.

        Article on a forthcoming appearance by Malcolm at
        the Democratic Club of Harlem, as part of a series of
        speeches on "The Negro Revolution." (50)

4B-77   "Harlem Is Bracing for Muslim Rally." Amsterdam News,
        29 June 1963, p. 1.

        Story on a forthcoming rally to focus on drugs in
        the Afro-American community. Malcolm is listed as the
        main speaker and the article notes that the Muslims
        are known for drawing the largest crowds in Harlem.
        (200)

4B-78   "A White Christian Looks at Black Muslims, pt. 2."
        Amsterdam News, 6 July 1963, p. 10.

        Continuation of citation 4B-74. He criticizes
        Muslims for being absent from the civil rights
        movement. (500)

4B-79   "Malcolm X Scores JFK's Trip Abroad." Amsterdam News,
        6 July 1963, p. 22.

        Report on a speech in which Malcolm criticizes
        Kennedy for being more concerned about European
        affairs than issues confronting the Afro-American
        community. (100)

4B-80   "5,000 Hear New York Muslims." Muhammad Speaks, 19
        July 1963, p. 21.

        Story of a rally addressed by Malcolm, where he
        calls for a moral reformation in the Afro-American
        community. (250)

4B-81   "116th Street Rally." Amsterdam News, 13 July 1963,
        p. 8.

        Picture of Malcolm addressing a rally in Harlem at
        which 2,000 attended. (30)

4B-82   "Muslims Set Saturday Rally Uptown." Amsterdam News,
        3 Aug 1963, p. 4.

        Note on a forthcoming rally. Malcolm quoted on the
        need for a "united black front" of Afro-American
        organizations. (75)

4B-83   "March (on Washington) 'Impressed' Malcolm X."
        Amsterdam News, 7 Sept 1963, p. 6.

        Malcolm quoted as saying the march was impressive
        just as the World Series is impressive. Called it a
        circus which accomplished nothing. (250)

4B-84   "Malcolm X to Speak in Harlem." Amsterdam News, 7
        Sept 1963, p. 20.

        Note on a forthcoming Nation of Islam rally. (50)

4B-85   "Malcolm X Back, Will Speak Friday." Amsterdam News,
        19 Oct 1963, p. 7.

        Notes return of Malcolm to New York after speaking
        engagements in California. (100)

4B-86   "Powell and Mr. X Blackjack Bunche." Amsterdam News,
        2 Nov 1963, p. 1.

        Responses of Malcolm and Powell to criticism from
        Ralph Bunche. Malcolm's response is that he should
        attack white racists and not other Afro-Americans.
        (250)

4B-87   "Malcolm X and Adam Powell." Amsterdam News, 16 Nov
        1963, p. 11.

Column by Jackie Robinson on the Bunche-Malcolm exchange. Robinson criticizes Malcolm and Powell for not being on the front lines of the civil rights movement. (400)

4B-88 "Malcolm and Bunche Respond to Robinson Editorial." Amsterdam News, 30 Nov 1963, p. 1.

Two letters. The letter from Bunche to Robinson criticizes Powell and Malcolm and lists his own credentials in the civil rights movement. Malcolm's letter counterposes the fate of Robinson to the fate of Paul Robeson. He accuses Robinson of trying to please whites by attacking him. (1000)

4B-89 "Malcolm X Suspended for JFK Remarks." Amsterdam News, 7 Dec 1963, p. 1.

Story on Malcolm's suspension. Includes quotes from Malcolm's remarks that led to the suspension and his remarks agreeing to the justness of the suspension. Also includes the text of the telegram from Elijah Muhammad ordering the suspension. (300)

4B-90 "Jackie Robinson Again Writes to Malcolm X." Amsterdam News, 14 Dec 1963, p. 1.

Open letter to Malcolm answering the attack upon him by Malcolm. (500)

4B-91 "Malcolm X Maintains Silence." Amsterdam News, 14 Dec 1963, p. 54.

Article on Malcolm's activities. He is reported to be handling administrative responsibilities in the New York Mosque. Other ministers are filling in on speaking engagements. (250)

4B-92 "I Hate You." Amsterdam News, 14 Dec 1963, p. 13.

Column by Gertrude Wilson in which she states that Malcolm's remarks following the Kennedy assassination were misunderstood. (250)

4B-93   "Nation Still Mourns Kennedy Death." Muhammad Speaks,
        20 Dec 1963, p. 1.

        Message from Elijah Muhammad on Kennedy's death.
        Includes a statement confirming Malcolm's suspension
        from public speaking for an "indefinite period." (600)

4B-94   "Muhammad's Statement on the President's Death."
        Muhammad Speaks, 20 Dec 1963, p. 3.

        Press release from Elijah Muhammad stating
        Malcolm's suspension from public speaking. (200)

4B-95   "Malcolm X Is Still Suspended." Amsterdam News, 4 Ja
        1964, p. 1.

        Note that Malcolm's suspension is still in effect
        for an undetermined period. (50)

4B-96   "Malcolm X in Florida." Amsterdam News, 25 Ja 1964,
        p. 1.

        Note that Malcolm and his family are vacationing in
        Miami as guests of Cassius Clay. (50)

4B-97   "Bar Malcolm from Muslims' Chicago Convention."
        Amsterdam News, 15 Feb 1964, p. 1.

        Note that Malcolm would not be attending the annual
        convention of the Nation of Islam. (200)

4B-98   "Malcolm X 'Comeback' in March." Amsterdam News, 22
        Feb 1964, p. 1.

        Note that Malcolm is expected to resume his full
        duties in March. (150)

4B-99   "Nationalist Pleads for Malcolm X." Amsterdam News,
        29 Feb 1964, p. 3.

        Open telegram from Dr. Lewis Michaux to Elijah
        Muhammad, asking that the suspension of Malcolm be
        lifted. (300)

4B-100 "Telegram to Muhammad." Amsterdam News, 14 Mar 1964,
        p. 1.

        Exerpts from a telegram Malcolm sent to Elijah
        Muhammad. States that he is leaving the Nation of
        Islam because people around Muhammad are forcing him
        out. States his intention to continue to carry out
        Muhammad's program. (200)

4B-101 "Malcolm X: 'Why I Quit and What I Plan Next.'"
        Amsterdam News, 14 Mar 1964, p. 1.

        Article on the split. Malcolm contends he was
        forced out by jealous assistants to Muhammad. States
        that he intends to form a black nationalist group and
        carry out an "action program" based on the teaching of
        Elijah Muhammad. Includes a comment from Elijah
        Muhammad that he was "stunned" by the departure of
        Malcolm. (600)

4B-102 "Reckless Orbit." Amsterdam News, 14 Mar 1964, p. 12.

        Editorial on the split. Notes that Malcolm is
        destined to become even "wilder" in his public
        statements. (150)

4B-103 "Malcolm X Tells of Death Threat." Amsterdam News, 21
        Mar 1964, p. 50.

        A statement from Malcolm telling of some internal
        dissension in the New York Mosque. Tells of a plot to
        assassinate him and a campaign to question his mental
        balance. (650)

4B-104 "Malcolm X Explains His Rifle Statement." Amsterdam
        News, 28 Mar 1964, p. 35.

        Speech by Malcolm at a Harlem rent strike rally.
        Explains his views on self-defense, his willingness to
        work with other Afro-American organizations, and his
        idea that only a back-to-Africa movement can solve the
        racial problem. (400)

4B-105 "King Views Malcolm X as Tragic." Amsterdam News, 28
       Mar 1964, p. 35.

       Dr. King's response to Malcolm's call for self-
       defense. States that it would cause tragic
       consequences if violence were used. (30)

4B-106 "Malcolm X Visiting Senate; Hits Leaders." Amsterdam
       News, 28 Mar 1964, p. 50.

       Announcement that Malcolm X will visit D.C. to view
       the filibuster of the Civil Rights Act. States that
       he will get involved in the civil rights movement and
       intends to start a voter registration drive in New
       York City. (250)

4B-107 "Malcolm X Ignores Brother." Amsterdam News, 4 Apr
       1964, p. 1.

       Malcolm's brother accuses him of wanting to take
       the place of Elijah Muhammad and hints at Malcolm's
       mental instability. Malcolm responds that the Nation
       of Islam is worried because many of their followers
       have joined his movement. (300)

4B-108 "Malcolm: Exposed by His Brother." Muhammad Speaks,
       10 Apr 1964, p. 3.

       Text of a statement by Malcolm's brother. Accuses
       Malcolm of speaking falsely of the personal affairs of
       Elijah Muhammad and of disobeying his orders to remain
       silent about the Kennedy assassination. (500)

4B-109 "Organize Rifle Club in Ohio: Malcolm X on the
       Scene." Amsterdam News, 11 Apr 1964, p. 1.

       Article on a radio interview in Cleveland. Malcolm
       advises Afro-Americans to form rifle clubs for self-
       defense. (300)

4B-110 "Seek to Evict Malcolm X from Home in Queens."
       Amsterdam News, 18 Apr 1964, p. 1.

Story of the Nation of Islam's attempt to evict
Malcolm from his home. Includes a note of Malcolm's
plans to travel to Africa and the Middle East. (250)

4B-111 "Postpone Malcolm X Home Case." Amsterdam News, 25
Apr 1964, p. 1.

Note that the attempt to evict Malcolm was
postponed because he was traveling in Africa. (50)

4B-112 "Malcolm X in Brooklyn." Amsterdam News (Brooklyn
edition), 25 Apr 1964, p. 32.

Note of a speech by Malcolm at a church in
Brooklyn. States he intends to be an evangelist for
black nationalism. (100)

4B-113 "Minister Who Knew Him Best Rips Malcolm's Treachery,
pt. 1." Muhammad Speaks, 8 May 1964, p. 13.

Article by Louis Farrakhan (then Louis X) on
Malcolm. Criticizes Malcolm for speaking out on
Kennedy's assassination. States that Malcolm was not
pressured out of the Nation of Islam but quit of his
own will. (600)

4B-114 "Seek to Link Malcolm X to Slayings in Harlem."
Amsterdam News, 9 May 1964, p. 1.

Report that a Queens, N.Y. District Attorney was
attempting to link Malcolm's speeches to an outbreak
of racial violence in New York. (250)

4B-115 "Malcolm X Has New Name in Arabia." Amsterdam News, 9
May 1963, p. 62.

Report on Malcolm's name change to El-Haj Malik El
Shabazz. Also reports he has been the guest of Crown
Prince Faisal of Saudi Arabia. (150)

4B-116 "Is Mecca Trip Changing Malcolm?" Amsterdam News, 23
May 1964, p. 14.

Report of a letter received by the Amsterdam News from Malcolm in which he comments on the color-blind attitude of Islam. (300)

4B-117 "My Next Move: Malcolm X, An Exclusive Interview." Amsterdam News, 30 May 1964, p. 1.

Statement by Malcolm upon his return from Africa. He states his intention to set up a new Afro-American organization that all Afro-Americans would be able to join and points out that whites would be able to support it. (500)

4B-118 "Fall of a Minister." Muhammad Speaks, 5 June 1964, p. 8.

Second part of Louis Farrakhan's article. He accuses Malcolm of trying to paint himself as a prophet. (300)

4B-119 "Malcolm X Flees for Life; Muslim Factions at War." Amsterdam News, 20 June 1964, p. 1.

Report of a confrontation between Malcolm's supporters and members of the Nation of Islam. Report comments on the bad relations between the two groups. (300)

4B-120 "Muslim Factions Keep Fighting." Amsterdam News (Brooklyn edition), 27 June 1964, p. 1.

Note on more confrontations between the rival Muslim groups. Malcolm announces that he will form the Organization of Afro-American Unity (OAAU). (150)

4B-121 "Muslim Minister Writes to Malcolm." Muhammad Speaks, 3 July 1964, p. 9.

Open letter by a Muslim minister. Accuses Malcolm of having left Islam and putting his faith in guns. (500)

4B-122 "Muslims Rally to Muhammad." Amsterdam News, 4 July
       1964, p. 1.

       Report on a Muslim rally attracting 12,000 people,
       many from out of state. Malcolm comments that Elijah
       Muhammad should attack the Ku Klux Klan and not his
       organization. (400)

4B-123 "No 'Cheek Turning' Says Malcolm X." Amsterdam News,
       4 July 1964, p. 48.

       Report of a telegram Malcolm sent to Dr. King and
       James Foreman of SNCC. Malcolm writes his willingness
       to send some of his followers to the South in order to
       help organize self-defense squads. (200)

4B-124 "Ex-Sweetheart of Malcolm X Accuses Elijah." Amster-
       dam News, 11 July 1964, p. 1.

       Note on two paternity suits filed against Elijah
       Muhammad by two of his former secretaries, one an ex-
       girlfriend of Malcolm X. Also reports a radio program
       where Malcolm states that he is marked for
       assassination. (400)

4B-125 "Socialist Candidate for Malcolm." Amsterdam News, 18
       July 1964, p. 10.

       Statement of support for the OAAU by Clifton
       DeBarry, presidential candidate on the Socialist
       Workers Party ticket. (100)

4B-126 "Riddle of Malcolm X." Amsterdam News, 18 July 1964,
       p. 21.

       Editorial by Jackie Robinson criticizing Malcolm
       for his attacks on the civil rights leadership.
       Suggests that the OAAU will never go anywhere. (700)

4B-127 "Adam and Malcolm X Absent during Riots." Amsterdam
       News, 25 July 1964, p. 30.

       Note on Malcolm's absence during the Harlem riots.
       Mentions his presence in Cairo at an OAU meeting.
       (150)

4B-128 "Truth and Travails of a Righteous Prophet." Muhammad
        Speaks, 31 July 1964, p. 11.

        Article by Louis Farrakhan which contains a veiled
        threat to Malcolm. States that the Nation of Islam
        will not tolerate evil talk about Elijah Muhammad.
        (1000)

4B-129 "Fall of a Domestic Prophet." Muhammad Speaks, 14 Aug
        1964, p. 6.

        Article sent by a reader who asserts that Malcolm
        is going insane. Author affirms the correctness of
        Elijah Muhammad. (250)

4B-130 "Order Evictions of Malcolm X." Amsterdam News, 5
        Sept 1964, p. 1.

        Court finding that Malcolm's house was legally the
        property of the Nation of Islam. (100)

4B-131 "Memo: From the Desk of Muhammad." Muhammad Speaks,
        11 Sept 1964, p. 5.

        In the context of a long Bible-quoting article,
        Elijah Muhammad accuses Malcolm of being a hypocrite
        and of trying to spread slander against him. He also
        accuses Malcolm of using his (Malcolm's) ex-girl-
        friends to falsely charge him with moral offenses.
        (1500)

4B-132 "Why Muslims Will Never Be Fooled by the False."
        Muhammad Speaks, 11 Sept 1964, p. 8.

        Article by a Muslim minister counseling people not
        to follow Malcolm. (400)

4B-133 "Vicious Scheming and Treachery by Malcolm X."
        Muhammad Speaks, 25 Sept 1964, p. 4.

        Short article by a Muslim minister on Malcolm.
        (150)

4B-134 "Biography of a Hypocrite, pt. 1." Muhammad Speaks,
       25 Sept 1964, p. 16.

       Article by two Muslim ministers. Accuses Malcolm
       of having been a petty thief who used Islam to get out
       of prison early. (500)

4B-135 "Biography of a Hypocrite, pt. 2." Muhammad Speaks, 9
       Oct 1964, p. 5.
            .
       Accuses Malcolm of falsely claiming to have founded
       the East Coast Mosques of the Nation of Islam.
       Accuses him of practicing deception and carrying
       dissension every place he went. (400)

4B-136 "Minister Warns Muslims Against False Leaders."
       Muhammad Speaks, 9 Oct 1964, p. 11.

       Article accusing the press of trying to build up
       Malcolm as a leader. (500)

4B-137 "Malcolm X to Open Center Here." Amsterdam News, 17
       Oct 1964, p. 3.

       Note that Malcolm will open a Muslim Center in New
       York upon his return from Africa. Also quotes a
       report that Malcolm sent a letter from Africa
       denouncing racism in any form. (150)

4B-138 "Malcolm-Muhammad's Biggest Hypocrite." Muhammad
       Speaks, 4 Dec 1964, p. 11.

       Long article by Louis Farrakhan accusing Malcolm of
       using religion and politics to attack Elijah Muhammad.
       Criticizes Malcolm for his trips to Africa and accuses
       Malcolm of attempting to use women to attack Elijah
       Muhammad. (2500)

4B-139 "Malcolm X In, Out to London." Amsterdam News, 5 Dec
       1964, p. 4.

       Note on Malcolm's return from a five-month stay in
       Africa. He tells of his intentions to visit the South

and his willingness to work with other civil rights organizations. (250)

4B-140 "Malcolm X to Show Film on Africa." Amsterdam News, 2 Ja 1965, p. 12.

Announcement of a program sponsored by the OAAU. Film to be shown was of Malcolm's five-month trip to Africa. (75)

4B-141 "Malcolm X to Speak at Palm Gardens." Amsterdam News, 2 Ja 1964, p. 14.

Announcement of a forthcoming speech by Malcolm on "1965: The Prospects for Freedom." (30)

4B-142 "Victory of the Apostle." Muhammad Speaks, 15 Ja 1965, p. 1.

Article by Elijah Muhammad on the fate of hypocrites. Consists mostly of quotes from the Bible and the Koran. (1000)

4B-143 "Malcolm: Exposed by His Brother." Muhammad Speaks, 15 Ja 1965, p. 15.

Reprint of citation 4B-108.

4B-144 "Muslim Factions at War." Amsterdam News, 16 Ja 1965, p. 1.

Speech by Cassius Clay at a Muslim dinner where he accuses Malcolm of believing the press hype he received as a Muslim minister. (150)

4B-145 "Malcolm Warns American Nazis." Amsterdam News, 23 Ja 1965, p. 43.

Telegram sent by Malcolm to George Lincoln Rockwell, leader of the American Nazi Party, threatening the Nazis with physical retaliation if Dr. King or other civil rights workers are harmed. (100)

4B-146 "Muslim Minister Blasts Malcolm X." Amsterdam News,
        30 Ja 1965, p. 6.

        Speech by a New York Muslim minister in which he
        calls Malcolm a hypocrite. Malcolm's response is not
        to get involved in verbal debates with the Nation of
        Islam. Article details the status of Leon Ameer, an
        associate of Malcolm's, and Akbar Muhammad, Elijah's
        son, who also quit the Nation of Islam. (600)

4B-147 "March on Under Messenger's Banner." Muhammad Speaks,
        5 Feb 1965, p. 4.

        Article by a Pakistani Muslim, affiliated with the
        Nation of Islam, accusing Malcolm of maintaining his
        criminal mentality of a pimp. (400)

4B-148 "Malcolm X Speaks." Amsterdam News, 6 Feb 1965, p. 1.

        Article in which Malcolm charges that members of
        the Nation of Islam have attempted to assassinate
        him. Also mentions his plans to speak to several
        civil rights groups in Alabama and Mississippi. (600)

4B-149 "Convict Muslims in Boston." Amsterdam News, 6 Feb
        1965, p. 1.

        Conviction of several members of the Nation of
        Islam for assaulting Leon Ameer, an associate of
        Malcolm's. (200)

4B-150 "I'm Ready to Meet the Challenges of the Messenger's
        Foes." Muhammad Speaks, 12 Feb 1965, p. 4.

        Article by a Pakistani Muslim, affiliated with the
        Nation of Islam, who accuses Malcolm of setting up
        organizations to contend with the Nation of Islam and
        of attempting to create discord within the ranks of
        the Nation of Islam. (400)

4B-151 "Malcolm X to Reveal New Plans." Amsterdam News, 13
        Feb 1965, p. 5.

Announcement of an OAAU meeting in which Malcolm will announce an "action program" to combat the social ills of the Afro-American community. (50)

4B-152 "Malcolm Denies He Is Bomber." Amsterdam News (Brooklyn edition), 20 Feb 1965, p. 1.

Statement by Malcolm that Elijah Muhammad ordered the bombing of his house. (200)

4B-153 "Malcolm Died Broke." Amsterdam News, 27 Feb 1965, p. 1.

Note on Malcolm's finances and details of a fund-raising committee set up by Ossie Davis, Ruby Dee, and Abby Lincoln to raise money for Malcolm's wife, Betty Shabazz. (200)

4B-154 "Malcolm Will Get Islamic Burial." Amsterdam News, 27 Feb 1965, p. 1.

Note on the observance of Islamic burial rites for Malcolm's funeral. (200)

4B-155 "Malcolm X as 'the People' Knew Him." Amsterdam News, 27 Feb 1965, pp. 1, 3.

Series of three articles by Amsterdam News reporters George Barnes, Tony Bryce, and George Todd. All three detail their personal association with Malcolm. (1200)

4B-156 "Malcolm's Funeral Services." Amsterdam News, 27 Feb 1965, p. 1.

Note on the funeral arrangements for Malcolm. Article notes that several Afro-American churches refused the use of their premises for the funeral for fear of violence erupting at the services. (150)

4B-157 "Muslim Fire: Retaliation or Arson?" Amsterdam News, 27 Feb 1965, p. 1.

Article on the burning of the Nation of Islam's
Mosque in Harlem. Authorities determined that the
fire was deliberately set. (250)

4B-158 "Steady Eddie." Amsterdam News, 27 Feb 1965, p. 1.

An editorial appealing for calm in the wake of
Malcolm's assassination. (500)

4B-159 "Trust Fund for Malcolm X Kids." Amsterdam News, 27
Feb 1965, p. 1.

Note on the establishment of a trust fund to
finance the education of Malcolm's children. (100)

4B-160 "United Council to Meet." Amsterdam News, 27 Feb
1965, p. 1.

Note on the meeting of a coalition of Harlem
organizations to issue a plea for community stability,
an end to violence among rival organizations, and an
expression of horror over Malcolm's assassination.
(100)

4B-161 "Malcolm X: Many Things to Many People." Amsterdam
News, 27 Feb 1965, p. 7.

Photo essay showing Malcolm meeting with local,
national, and international dignitaries.

4B-162 "Malcolm X." Amsterdam News, 27 Feb 1965, p. 9.

Column by James Hicks giving personal reminiscences
of his relationship to Malcolm. (500)

4B-163 "Mrs. Malcolm X, 'A Friend of Mine.'" Amsterdam News,
27 Feb 1965, p. 9.

Column by Gertrude Wilson telling of her personal
relationship with Malcolm. Found Malcolm a warm and
compassionate man despite his public reputation.
(1000)

4B-164 "Playwright Discusses the Death of Malcolm X."
       Amsterdam News, 27 Feb 1965, p. 16.

       Article by Lofton Miller discussing the changes in
       Malcolm's political views. He views Malcolm as a
       victim of the permeation of violence in U.S. society.
       (700)

4B-165 "'Somebody' Was After Malcolm X." Amsterdam News, 27
       Feb 1965, p. 19.

       Article alleging that Malcolm was under constant
       surveillance by members of the Nation of Islam. (150)

4B-166 "Baldwin: Malcolm's Death Is a Setback." Amsterdam
       News, 27 Feb 1965, p. 20.

       Statement by James Baldwin asserting that Malcolm
       was the victim of a climate of racial hatred. (250)

4B-167 "What Harlemites Say about Malcolm X Slaying."
       Amsterdam News, 27 Feb 1965, p. 22.

       Ten short statements by average Harlemites on
       Malcolm's assassination. All sympathize with Malcolm.
       (400)

4B-168 "Malcolm X Helped Stranded Workers." Amsterdam News
       (Brooklyn edition), 27 Feb 1965, p. 1.

       Story of how Malcolm assisted a group of women
       brought to Harlem from the South to work as domestics.
       (400)

4B-169 Malcolm Told Cops of Plot to Kill Him." Amsterdam
       News (Brooklyn edition), 27 Feb 1965, p. 47.

       Article citing rumors that Malcolm had given
       detailed information to police on those who he
       suspected would try to kill him. (200)

4B-170 "Les Mathews and Malcolm X." Amsterdam News (Brooklyn edition), 27 Feb 1965, p. 47.

Personal reminiscences of an Amsterdam News reporter who knew Malcolm. (400)

4B-171 "The Speech Malcolm Wanted to Make." Amsterdam News (Brooklyn edition), 27 Feb 1965, p. 47.

Notes that Malcolm was never able to deliver the speech in which he was to explain the plan of action for the OAAU. (300)

4B-172 "Cathy White and Malcolm X." Amsterdam News (Brooklyn edition), 27 Feb 1965, p. 47.

Personal recollections of an Amsterdam News reporter who knew Malcolm. She relates a conversation she had with him while picketing a construction site. (400)

4B-173 "Malcolm Was Going to Mississippi." Amsterdam News (Brooklyn edition), 27 Feb 1965, p. 47.

Notes that Malcolm had planned to address the Mississippi Freedom Democratic Party on the week that he was assassinated. (50)

4B-174 "Indict Four Black Muslims for Assault." Amsterdam News (Brooklyn edition), 27 Feb 1965, p. 48.

Notes the indictment of several Nation of Islam members on a series of unrelated assaults. Includes the indictment of Norman Butler and Thomas Johnson, soon to be convicted of murdering Malcolm, on charges of shooting an ex-Muslim who was attempting to organize his own religious group. (150)

4B-175 "R. F. Williams Hits Attempts to Link Him with Malcolm's Death." Muhammad Speaks, 5 Mar 1965, p. 6.

Article quoting Williams' disavowal of any connection with Malcolm's assassination. (200)

4B-176 "Demise of Malcolm." Muhammad Speaks, 5 Mar 1965, p.
       9.

       Article by a Pakistani Muslim, affiliated with the
       Nation of Islam, telling of his hopes for a reconcili-
       ation between Malcolm and Elijah Muhammad. States
       that the Nation of Islam was not connected to the
       crime of Malcolm's murder. Views Malcolm's death as a
       result of the path he followed. (600)

4B-177 "Ossie Davis Stirring Tribute to Malcolm X."
       Amsterdam News, 6 Mar 1965, p. 1.

       Text of Ossie Davis' eulogy to Malcolm. (1000)

4B-178 "Mrs. Malcolm X Fund Now at $4,000." Amsterdam News,
       6 Mar 1965, p. 2.

       Note on the progress of the Malcolm X Fund. Notes
       that a benefit is being planned. (200)

4B-179 "Church Says it Did Not Refuse Malcolm." Amsterdam
       News, 6 Mar 1965, p. 2.

       Note that a church, identified by the Amsterdam
       News as having refused to hold Malcolm's services on
       their premises, was never asked to hold the service.
       (150)

4B-180 "Malcolm's Secretary Decries Open Warfare." Amsterdam
       News, 6 Mar 1965, p. 3.

       James Shabazz, an assistant to Malcolm, claims that
       "racist elements" in the U.S. government were behind
       Malcolm's assassination. (250)

4B-181 "How I Got to Know Malcolm Intimately." Amsterdam
       News, 6 Mar 1965, p. 3.

       Article by Amsterdam News reporter James Booker, in
       which he details his past association with Malcolm.
       States his respect for Malcolm as a leader. (500)

4B-182 "Malcolm X's Followers Follow Him to Grave."
Amsterdam News, 6 Mar 1965, p. 4.

Photo essay of Malcolm's burial.

4B-183 "Militant Labor Forum to Hold Malcolm X Service."
Amsterdam News, 6 Mar 1965, p. 6.

Announcement of a memorial meeting sponsored by the
Socialist Workers Party. (30)

4B-184 "Pat on the Back." Amsterdam News, 6 Mar 1965, p. 8.

An editorial congratulating Harlem for not rioting
in response to the assassination of Malcolm. (500)

4B-185 "No Time for Avengers." Amsterdam News, 6 Mar 1965,
p. 8.

Column by Roy Wilkins arguing against further
violence between rival Muslim groups. (600)

4B-186 "Next Malcolm X." Amsterdam News, 6 Mar 1965, p. 8.

Column by Whitney Young viewing Malcolm as arising
from the poverty and despair Afro-Americans face in
Harlem. (600)

4B-187 "Black Manhood." Amsterdam News, 6 Mar 1965, p. 9.

Column by James Hicks calling on Afro-American men
to be as proud and "manly" as Malcolm was. (500)

4B-188 "Look Homeward, Mr. Rowan." Amsterdam News, 6 Mar
1965, p. 9.

Column by Gertrude Wilson critical of Carl Rowan's
statement that Malcolm was a dope peddler and a racial
fanatic. Wilson points out that Malcolm rose above
his past. (500)

4B-189 "30,000 Mourn Malcolm X." Amsterdam News (Brooklyn
        edition), 6 Mar 1965, p. 35.

        Article on the funeral of Malcolm. (1000)

4B-190 "Setting the Record Straight." Muhammad Speaks, 12
        Mar 1965, p. 9.

        Article citing death threats against Elijah
        Muhammad. States that whites are using Malcolm's
        death just as they used his defection, to cause
        disunity. (700)

4B-191 "Who Sent 10G Check to Malcolm X Slaying Suspect."
        Amsterdam News, 13 Mar 1965, p. 1.

        Article noting that someone sent a $10,000 check to
        Norman Butler, while he was in jail, with a note
        saying it was for a "job well done." (400)

4B-192 "Indicted in Slaying." Amsterdam News, 13 Mar 1965,
        p. 2.

        Notes that Norman Butler, Talmadge Hayer, and
        Thomas Johnson were indicted for the murder of
        Malcolm. (50)

4B-193 "Lawyer Says Malcolm Was Poisoned." Amsterdam News,
        13 Mar 1965, p. 4.

        Allegation by an attorney and associate of
        Malcolm's, Milton Henry, that Malcolm was poisoned
        while he was in Cairo. (500)

4B-194 "Malcolm X Fund Grows to $5,200." Amsterdam News, 13
        Mar 1965, p. 4.

        Progress of the Malcolm X Fund.

4B-195 "Malcolm's Muslims Meet; Map Program." Amsterdam
        News, 13 Mar 1965, p. 4.

Notes that James Shabazz will assume leadership of
the Muslim Mosque, Inc., and Ella Collins, Malcolm's
sister, will assume leadership of the OAAU. (400)

4B-196 "Markings on Malcolm's Grave." Amsterdam News, 13 Mar
1965, p. 4.

Note on the inscription on the grave of Malcolm.
(150)

4B-197 "Muslim Factions Meet in Accord." Amsterdam News, 13
Mar 1965, p. 4.

Note on a meeting between members of the Nation of
Islam and several followers of Malcolm. (400)

4B-198 "Talk with Mrs. Malcolm X." Amsterdam News, 13 Mar
1965, p. 4.

Article based on an interview with Betty Shabazz.
She criticizes the white media for its misrepresenta-
tion of Malcolm. (500)

4B-199 "How World Saw Malcolm X's Death." Amsterdam News, 13
Mar 1965, p. 6.

Notes reaction of international press to the assassination. It received wide coverage in Africa and the
Middle East. (500)

4B-200 "Nightmare of Violence." Amsterdam News, 13 Mar 1965,
p. 10.

Column by Dr. King viewing Malcolm as a product of
hate and despair. Notes that with Malcolm's death the
world lost a potentially great leader. (600)

4B-201 "Someone Said." Amsterdam News, 13 Mar 1965, p. 10.

Editorial viewing Malcolm's death as a tragic
occurrence. (150)

4B-202 "Distressed at Coverage." Amsterdam News, 13 Mar
       1965, p. 10.

       Letter to the editor by A. S. "Doc" Young, an Afro-
       American journalist, criticizing the Amsterdam News
       for their positive coverage of Malcolm. (1000)

4B-203 "Press Bias Shows in Stories on Muslim Confab."
       Muhammad Speaks, 19 Mar 1965, p. 9.

       Criticism of press coverage for its inaccurate
       counting of numbers present at the annual Nation of
       Islam meeting. (400)

4B-204 "Malcolm X's Sister Takes Over." Amsterdam News, 20
       Mar 1965, p. 8.

       Notes that Ella Collins is taking over leadership
       of the OAAU. (200)

4B-205 "Malcolm X Widow Gets $500 Gift." Amsterdam News, 20
       Mar 1965, p. 26.

       Story of a gift from Shirley G. DuBois. (150)

4B-206 "Defends Race." Amsterdam News (Brooklyn edition), 20
       Mar 1965, p. 55.

       Letter to the editor attacking A. S. Young's
       criticism of Malcolm. Calls Young an Uncle Tom.
       (200)

4B-207 "Hits Doc Young." Amsterdam News (Brooklyn edition),
       20 Mar 1965, p. 55.

       Letter to the editor calling Young misled by white
       media distortions of Malcolm. (100)

4B-208 "Degrading." Amsterdam News (Brooklyn edition), 20
       Mar 1965, p. 55.

Letter to the editor calling Young's article a disgrace to Afro-Americans. (100)

4B-209 "Live Forever." Amsterdam News (Brooklyn edition), 20 Mar 1965, p. 55.

Letter to the editor attacking Young's letter. Calls Malcolm a true leader. (75)

4B-210 "Tragic Loss." Amsterdam News (Brooklyn edition), 20 Mar 1965, p. 55.

Letter to the editor decrying Malcolm's assassination. (200)

4B-211 "Not Yet." Amsterdam News (Brooklyn edition), 20 Mar 1965, p. 55.

Letter to the editor asking about the availability of Malcolm's autobiography. (30)

4B-212 "History Will Judge." Amsterdam News (Brooklyn edition), 20 Mar 1965, p. 55.

Letter to the editor on Malcolm's contributions. (200)

4B-213 "Malcolm Spoke Out." Amsterdam News (Brooklyn edition), 20 Mar 1965, p. 55.

Letter to the editor from a white minister who asserts that Malcolm spoke for many Afro-Americans. (200)

4B-214 "Muslim Leadership Undecided." Amsterdam News, 27 Mar 1965, p. 1.

Report on a group of OAAU members who challenged Ella Collins' right to lead the organization. (300)

4B-215 "Real Malcolm X." Amsterdam News, 28 Mar 1965, p. 11.

Text of a letter written by Malcolm to Amsterdam
News reporter James Booker, from Ghana in May 1964.
In the letter Malcolm advocates Pan-Africanism. (500)

4B-216 "Brilliant But Bitter." Amsterdam News, 3 Apr 1965,
p. 18.

Letter to the Editor finding Malcolm a brilliant
orator but bitter to the point of self-destruction.
(300)

4B-217 "Time Will Tell." Amsterdam News, 3 Apr 1965, p. 18.

Letter to the Editor seeing a conspiracy behind
Malcolm's assassination. (60)

4B-218 "Rips Rowan's Stand." Amsterdam News, 3 Apr 1965, p.
18.

Letter to the Editor attacking Carl Rowan for his
negative views of Malcolm. (150)

4B-219 "Beautiful Writing." Amsterdam News, 3 Apr 1965, p.
18.

Letter to the Editor congratulating the Amsterdam
News for its writing on Malcolm. (50)

4B-220 "Mrs. Malcolm X Pens Us a Note." Amsterdam News, 10
Apr 1965, p. 2.

On a note to the Amsterdam News from Betty Shabazz,
written while on a pilgrimage to Mecca. (100)

4B-221 "Now Understands." Amsterdam News, 10 Apr 1965, p.
16.

Letter to the Editor expressing understanding of
Malcolm's views in light of the violence against civil
rights workers in Selma, Ala. (100).

4B-222 "An Ill Wind." Amsterdam News, 10 Apr 1965, p. 16.

Letter to the Editor critical of Carl Rowan for his comments on Malcolm. (400)

4B-223 "Tribute to Malcolm." Amsterdam News, 17 Apr 1965, p. 14.

Letter to the Editor praising Malcolm as courageous. (250)

4B-224 "Martyred Champion." Amsterdam News, 17 Apr 1965, p. 14.

Letter to the Editor viewing Malcolm's loss as devastating for the poor, who have lost their only spokesman. (250)

4B-225 "Protection." Amsterdam News, 17 Apr 1965, p. 14.

Letter to the Editor questioning why Malcolm wasn't given adequate police protection. (25)

4B-226 "Benefit for Malcolm X Widow Friday Nite." Amsterdam News, 24 Apr 1965, p. 26.

Announcement of a benefit featuring Ossie Davis, Nina Simone, Sammy Davis, and others. (300)

4B-227 "Threat to Mrs. X. Benefit." Amsterdam News, 1 May 1965, p. 1.

Note of a bomb threat at a benefit for Betty Shabazz. (250)

4B-228 "Mrs. X Back, Has No Plans." Amsterdam News, 8 May 1965, p. 1.

Note on Betty Shabazz's return from Mecca. Mentions that she has no intention of taking part in the activities of the OAAU. (200)

4B-229 "Festival for Mrs. X." Amsterdam News, 24 July 1965,
　　　p. 1.

　　　Announcement of a benefit for Betty Shabazz. (300)

4B-230 "Malcom X Murder Is Unsolved." Amsterdam News, 31
　　　July 1965, p. 1.

　　　Notes that there are many unanswered questions
　　about Malcolm's assassination. (400)

4B-231 "Aid Mrs. Malcolm X Buy New Home." Amsterdam News, 14
　　　Aug 1965, p. 1.

　　　Note on Betty Shabazz's purchase of a new home with
　　funds raised from benefits. (200)

4B-232 "See Early Trial in Malcolm." Amsterdam News, 21 Aug
　　　1965, p. 1.

　　　On an announcement from the District Attorney's
　　office that the trial would begin in the fall. (300)

4B-233 "Twins Born to Mrs. Malcolm X." Amsterdam News, 9 Oct
　　　1965, p. 1.

　　　(100)

4B-234 "Malcolm X Trial for Three Scheduled." Amsterdam
　　　News, 20 Nov 1965, p. 1.

　　　Announcement of trial date for Dec. 6, 1965. Notes
　　some criticism from community groups on the slow pace
　　of the trial. (200)

4B-235 "Protect Malcolm X Jurors." Amsterdam News, 22 Ja
　　　1966, p. 1.

　　　Summary of probable defense and prosecution
　　strategies. (500)

4B-236 "Who's Who at Malcolm X Trial." Amsterdam News, 22 Ja
       1966, p. 2.

       Listing of defendants, prosecutors, and defense
       attorneys. (250)

4B-237 "Jury Picked in Trial." Amsterdam News, 22 Ja 1966,
       p. 2.

       Listing of twelve jurors, giving their names and
       occupations. (250)

4B-238 "To Discuss Malcolm X." Amsterdam News, 22 Ja 1966,
       p. 2.

       Announcement of a five-hour call-in radio talk show
       to be devoted to discussing Malcolm X. (100)

4B-239 "What Malcolm X Trial Jurors Had to Answer."
       Amsterdam News, 29 Ja 1966, p. 2.

       Listing of questions asked of prospective jurors.
       (300)

4B-240 "Daily Capsule of Malcolm X Trial." Amsterdam News,
       29 Ja 1966, p. 2.

       Daily summary of trial proceedings. (2000)

4B-241 "Malcolm X Murder Trial." Amsterdam News, 5 Feb 1966,
       p. 1.

       Testimony of a Malcolm X aide on Malcolm's
       suspicion that both the Nation of Islam and the "power
       structure" wanted him dead. (400)

4B-242 "Daily Capsule in Malcolm Trial." Amsterdam News, 5
       Feb 1966, p. 2.

       Daily summary of trial proceedings. (2000)

4B-243 "They Knew Malcolm X." Amsterdam News, 5 Feb 1966, p. 13.

  Column by Gertrude Wilson on attendance at the trial. (500)

4B-244 "Malcolm X Trial Setting Precedents." Amsterdam News, 12 Feb 1966, p. 1.

  On barring the press and public during the testimony of a "mystery witness." Article points out some of the contradictory testimony that has been heard. (1000)

4B-245 "I'll Tell It All: Malcolm X's Widow." Amsterdam News, 19 Feb 1966, p. 1.

  On Betty Shabazz's decision to testify at the trial. Article also reviews her life since the assassination. (500)

4B-246 "When Malcolm Died." Amsterdam News, 19 Feb 1966, p. 1.

  Questions whether the truth will ever be known about the assassination. (200)

4B-247 "Daily Capsule in Malcolm X Trial." Amsterdam News, 19 Feb 1966, p. 2.

  Daily summary of trial proceedings. (250)

4B-248 "Malcolm Memorial." Amsterdam News, 19 Feb 1966, p. 2.

  Announcement of a memorial service. (50)

4B-249 "When Malcolm X Died." Amsterdam News, 19 Feb 1966, p. 47.

  Detailed summary of the medical testimony describing Malcolm's wounds. (1000)

4B-250 "Defense on in Trial." Amsterdam News, 26 Feb 1966,
       p. 1.

       Summary of the prosecution's case. (1000)

4B-251 "Ossie Davis in Tribute to Malcolm." Amsterdam News,
       26 Feb 1966, p. 1.

       On a memorial tribute addressed by Ossie Davis.
       Mentions a memorial march that was held that attracted
       75 people. (200)

4B-252 "Daily Capsule in Malcolm X Trial." Amsterdam News,
       26 Feb 1966, p. 2.

       Daily summary of trial proceedings. (2000)

4B-253 "I Killed Malcolm: Hagan." Amsterdam News, 5 Mar
       1966, p. 1.

       On Hayer's [Hagan's] confession. (600)

4B-254 "Daily Capsule in Malcolm X Trial." Amsterdam News, 5
       Mar 1966, p. 2.

       Daily summary of trial proceedings. (2000)

4B-255 "Malcolm X Trial to Jury." Amsterdam News, 12 Mar
       1966, p. 3.

       Summary of trial. (500)

4B-256 "Malcolm Honored in Graveside Rites." Amsterdam News,
       28 May 1966, p. 6.

       Story of a memorial sponsored by the OAAU. (250)

4B-257 "FBI Plot to Crush Black Struggle." Burning Spear,
       Apr 1974, p. 13.

       Article based on FBI files. Claims Malcolm's body-
       guard was an FBI informant. (800)

4B-258 "Nation of Islam to Rename Temple after Malcolm."
       Black Panther, 14 Feb 1976, p. 9.

       Story of the Nation of Islam's plans to rename
       their New York Mosque after Malcolm. Also mentions
       changes in racial and political philosophy of the
       Nation of Islam. (500)

4B-259 "El-Hajj Malik El Shabazz Profiled." Bilalian News,
       17 Mar 1978, p. 10.

       Short profile of Malcolm with excerpts from one of
       his letters from Mecca reflecting his changed racial
       views.

4B-260 "Who Killed Malcolm X?" Black News, Feb 1979, p. 6.

       Part one of an interview with Norman Butler who
       denies being at the scene of the assassination. Indi-
       cates his knowledge of police agents in the audience
       and among Malcolm's staff. (2000)

4B-261 "The Accused Assassin Speaks Out." Black News, Mar-
       Apr 1979, p. 12.

       Part two of the interview with Butler. He comments
       on prison life and the lack of support for him from
       the Nation of Islam.

4B-262 "Interview: Malcolm's Confessed Assassin." Black
       News, Mar-Apr 1980, p. 8.

       Interview with Hayer. He admits his guilt in the
       assassination which included two other accomplices,
       not the men convicted. Says he was promised money but
       did it because Malcolm slandered Elijah Muhammad.

4B-263 "Wrong Men Jailed in Malcolm Slaying?" Bilalian News,
       7 Mar 1980, p. 2.

       Copy of a petition submitted by Butler and Johnson
       to Congress asking that an investigation of Malcolm's
       assassination be opened. Petition lists their alibis
       and summarizes new evidence. (2000)

4B-264 "Muhammad: Men Need New Day in Court." Bilalian News,
       7 Mar 1980, p. 2.

       Column by Wallace Muhammad stating his belief that
       Butler and Johnson are innocent. (1000)

4B-265 "Malcolm X and the Nation of Islam." World Muslim
       News, 9 Apr 1982, p. 5.

       Wallace Muhammad states that Malcolm left the
       Nation of Islam because of friction between Malcolm
       and the national staff. (500)

4B-266 "Defense Committee Works to Free Imam Iziz." American
       Muslim Journal, 25 Feb 1983, p. 6.

       Note on the formation of a defense committee to
       assist Butler (Aziz) in his attempts for a retrial.
       (200)

IVC   NEWS REPORTS--LEFT-WING PRESS

4C-1   "Muslim Leader Suspends Malcolm X from Making Any
         Public Statement." Militant, 16 Dec 1963, p. 2.

         Report of Malcolm's suspension from the Nation of
       Islam. (350)

4C-2   "Malcolm X Maps Campaign to Build Black Nationalism."
         Militant, 16 Mar 1964, p. 1.

         Report from an interview with Malcolm by the
       Militant. Includes lengthy quotes from Malcolm in
       which he states his views on civil rights, black
       nationalism, and voter registration. (850)

4C-3   "DeBerry Lauds Malcolm X's Stand." Militant, 16 Mar
         1964, p. 1.

         Statement by Clifton DeBerry, Socialist Workers
       Party candidate for President, in which he states
       agreement with Malcolm X on black nationalism, self-
       defense, and the civil rights movement. (200)

4C-4   "Malcolm X Says Group Will Stress Politics." National
         Guardian, 21 Mar 1964, p. 4.

         Report from an interview in which Malcolm gives his
       views on the strategy and program of his new organiza-
       tion, the Muslim Mosque Inc. Includes a responding
       comment from Elijah Muhammad. (1300)

4C-5   "Mrs. Richardson Hails Support of Malcolm X."
         National Guardian, 21 Mar 1964, p. 4.

         Report on a statement by Gloria Richardson, chair

of the Non-Violent Action Committee of Cambridge, MD, in which she welcolmes Malcolm's participation in the civil rights movement. (210)

4C-6   "Malcolm X Starts Movement in Harlem for All Negroes." Militant, 23 Mar 1964, p. 1.

Report from a press conference in which Malcolm states his plans to start a new mass organization in the Afro-American community. Includes quotes from Malcolm on self-defense, the Civil Rights Bill, and integration. (1500)

4C-7   "DeBerry Denounces Threat to Malcolm X by New York Cops." Militant, 23 Mar 1964, p. 6.

Article by DeBerry in which he accuses police officials of distorting Malcolm's words. He also attacks the police department's "get tough" campaign against civil rights groups. (850)

4C-8   "Malcolm X Speaks on Black Revolution." Militant, 23 Mar 1964, p. 6.

Advertisement for a speech by Malcolm sponsored by the Militant Labor Forum.

4C-9   "3,000 Cheer Malcolm X at Opening Rally in Harlem." Militant, 30 Apr 1964, p. 1.

Report on a mass rally called by Malcolm. In his speech Malcolm discusses school integration, black nationalism, the Civil Rights Bill, and bringing the Afro-American question before the U.N. Article includes comments from the reporter on the crowd's reaction.

4C-10   "New Force Can Bring Major Rights Gains." Militant, 30 Mar 1964, p. 3.

Analysis by George Breitman on the significance of Malcolm's break with the Nation of Islam. Breitman sees Malcolms becoming a positive force in the black nationalist movement. (2500)

4C-11   "Malcolm X and Old Radicals." News and Letters, Apr
        1964, p. 5.

        Article by Raya Dunayevskaya. She criticizes
        Malcolm's position on black nationalism and criticizes
        the Socialist Workers Party for their support of
        Malcolm. Views the significance of Malcolm's split
        from the Nation of Islam as a recognition that the
        Afro-American people reject racism of any kind. (1200)

4C-12   "Malcolm X Talk Schedule." National Guardian, 4 Apr
        1964, p. 3.

        News Item announcing a speech by Malcolm at the
        Militant Labor Forum. (60)

4C-13   "Malcolm X to Organize Mass Voter Registration."
        Militant, 6 Apr 1964, p. 1.

        Report on a statement by Malcolm about his plans to
        organize a voter registration drive in New York. He
        advocates registering as independents and comments
        that he is still following the teachings of Elijah
        Muhammad. (700)

4C-14   "His Stand Can Unite and Build Movement." Militant, 6
        Apr 1964, p. 3.

        Analysis by George Breitman on how Malcolm might
        become the central figure in revolutionary black
        nationalist politics. Lauds his position on self-
        defense, politics, and black unity. (3000)

4C-15   "2,000 Hear Malcolm X in Cleveland." Militant, 13 Apr
        1964, p. 1.

        Report on a speech Malcolm gave under the auspices
        of CORE. (The "Ballot or the Bullet" speech.) (2100)

4C-16   "The Outlook of Malcolm X." National Guardian, 18 Apr
        1964, p. 11.

        Report on a speech by Malcolm at the Militant Labor

Forum. Notes the positive reaction of the predomi-
nantly white audience and details Malcolm's views on
integration, voter registration, and the possibilities
of a bloodless revolution. (800)

4C-17 "Malcolm X Details Black Nationalist Views." Militant
        20 Apr 1964, p. 8.

        Report on Malcolm's "Black Revolution" speech.
        ·Includes reports of rallies addressed by Malcolm in
        New York and Detroit. (3000)

4C-18 "Going to U.N. Can Help, But It's No Cure-All."
        Militant 25 May 1964, p. 5.

        Article by George Breitman critical of Malcolm's
        U.N. strategy. Views the U.N. as, at best, a place to
        expose the hypocrisy of the U.S., but not as a vehicle
        for change. (3000)

4C-19 "Malcolm X's Letters to US Describe Welcome in
        Africa." Militant, 25 May 1964, p. 6.

        Short item on Malcolm's letters from Mecca and
        Africa. (200)

4C-20 "Malcolm X Back from Africa--Urges Black United
        Front." Militant 1 June 1964, p. 8.

        Report on a press conference. Malcolm comments on
        integration and a mass return to Africa by Afro-
        Americans. (500)

4C-21 "1,500 in Chicago Hear Debate by Malcolm, Louis
        Lomax." Militant, 8 June 1964, p. 2.

        Report on a debate. Malcolm quoted on Dixiecrats
        and a mass return to Africa by Afro-Americans. (300)

4C-22 "Cheering Harlem Rally Hears Malcolm X Rip US Racism."
        Militant, 15 June 1964, p. 1.

Report on an OAAU rally. Malcolm quoted a praising Ben Bella of Algeria and Nasser of Egypt. (300)

4C-23 "Malcolm X May Form New Revolutionary Group." Challenge 20 June 1964, p. 3.

Report on a rally. Malcolm quoted on the Nation of Islam and Pan-Africanism. (200)

4C-24 "Why Black Nationalism Upsets White Liberals." Militant, 22 June 1964, p. 5.

Article by Robert Vernon criticizing an article by James Wechsler (citation #3-150). Calls Wechsler unsupportive of working class Afro-Americans and only supporting middle class Afro-Americans. (3000)

4C-25 "Threats of Violence Reported Directed Against Malcolm X." Militant, 22 June 1964, p. 8.

Report of a court appearance by Malcolm where he is surrounded by bodyguards. Recounts incidents of harrassment by members of the Nation of Islam. (250)

4C-26 "Malcolm X Announces Rally to Launch New Organization." Militant, 29 June 1964, p. 1.

Report of a rally announcing his plans for the OAAU. (200)

4C-27 "Malcolm X Launches a New Organization." Militant, 13 July 1964, p. 1.

Report on the formation of the OAAU. (500)

4C-28 "Program of Organization of Afro-American Unity." Militant, 13 July 1964, p. 2.

Text of the OAAU program. See citation #1-2(3). (2500)

4C-29   "Malcolm Blames New York Police Tactics." Militant,
           27 July 1964, p. 2.

           Report of a statement by Malcolm, in Cairo, blaming
        police brutality for the Harlem riots. (100)

4C-30   "Malcolm X in Cairo Hits Both Goldwater and Johnson."
           Militant, 14 Sept 1964, p. 8.

           Excerpts from citation #1-5(7). (300)

4C-31   "Malcolm X Group Resumes Weekly Harlem Meetings."
           Militant, 8 Oct 1964, p. 5.

           Note that the OAAU will meet regularly now that
        Malcolm has returned from Africa. (100)

4C-32   "Malcolm X Will Distribute 35 Scholarships."
           Militant, 2 Nov 1964, p. 8.

           Announcement of scholarships to study in Cairo.
        (150)

4C-33   "Malcolm X Raps LBJ Aggression." Challenge, 1 Dec
           1964, p. 2.

           Report on a press conference upon Malcolm's return
        from Africa. He criticizes the U.S. for its actions
        in the Congo. (125)

4C-34   "Malcolm X Assails US Role in Congo." Militant, 7 Dec
           1964, p. 1.

           Same report as citation #4C-33. Also relates
        Malcolm's travel itinerary and the leaders he met with
        on his trip. (500)

4C-35   "Paris Meeting Hears Malcolm X." Militant, 7 Dec
           1964, p. 4.

           Lengthy quotes from citation #1-2(7). (1500)

4C-36 "Millions of Britons See Malcolm X in TV Broadcast of
       Debate at Oxford." Militant, 14 Dec 1964, p. 2.

       Report on a debate. Malcolm quoted on the U.S.
       role in the Congo. (500)

4C-37 "Malcolm + Babu." Challenge, 15 Dec 1964, p. 3.

       Announcement of a rally featuring Malcolm and
       Mohammed Babu of Tanzania. (50)

4C-38 "Harlem Rally Demands 'Hands Off Congo.'" Militant,
       21 Dec 1964, p. 1.

       Report on citation #1-5(10). (400)

4C-39 "Malcolm X to Address New York Forum." Militant, 21
       Dec 1964, p. 8.

       Item announcing an appearance at the Militant Labor
       Forum. (75)

4C-40 "Meetings in Harlem Hear Malcolm X and Fannie Lou
       Hamer." Militant, 28 Dec 1964, p. 1.

       Report on an OAAU meeting. Malcolm quoted on the
       Democratic Party. (500)

4C-41 "Is Malcolm X Clueing in Africans on U.S.?" Militant,
       11 Ja 1965, p. 8.

       Report on Malcolm's activities at the OAU meeting.
       (250)

4C-42 "Harlem Rally Blasts U.S. Role in Congo." Challenge,
       12 Ja 1965, p. S3.

       Report on the rally with Mohammed Babu. Malcolm is
       quoted on the causes of the Harlem riot. (400)

4C-43 "Malcolm X at Militant Labor Forum." *Militant*, 18 Ja
       1965, p. 12.

       Report and quotes from citation #1-5(12). (600)

4C-44 "Rockwell Gets Warning from Malcolm X." *Militant*, 1
       Feb 1965, p. 8.

       Report of a telegram sent by Malcolm to George
       Lincoln Rockwell of the American Nazi Party. Malcolm
       threatens reprisals if any civil rights workers are
       hurt. (200)

4C-45 "Malcolm X Will Present Program at Harlem Rally."
       Militant, 15 Feb 1965, p. 8.

       Announcement of an OAAU rally. (75)

4C-46 "Malcolm X Discusses Bombing of Home." *Militant*, 22
       Feb 1965, p. 2.

       Report on a speech in which Malcolm blames the
       Nation of Islam for bombing his home and attempting
       his assassination. (600)

4C-47 "Murder of Malcolm X." *National Guardian*, 27 Feb
       1965, p. 2.

       Editorial on the assassination. Notes that Malcolm
       was in the process of reevaluating his opinion on many
       political questions. (600)

4C-48 "Express Shock at Malcolm X Slaying." *Worker*, 28 Feb
       1965, p. 2.

       Reactions from James Farmer, Roy Wilkins, and
       Martin Luther King on Malcolm's assassination. (400)

4C-49 "Malcolm X." *Worker*, 28 Feb 1965, p. 3.

       Editorial calling the assassination an act of vio-
       lence against the Afro-American freedom struggle. (250)

4C-50 "Murder of Malcolm X a Cruel Blow to the Cause of
       Black Emancipation." Militant, 1 Mar 1965, p. 1.

       Editorial recounting Malcolm's life. Views his
       assassination as a setback for the Afro-American move-
       ment but is confident he will be replaced by other
       militant nationalists. (1000)

4C-51 "Malcolm's Last Meeting." Militant, 1 Mar 1965, p. 1.

       Eyewitness account of the assassination. (600)

4C-52 "DeBerry Sends Condolences to Malcolm's Widow."
       Militant, 1 Mar 1965, p. 1.

       Text of condolences from DeBerry on behalf of the
       Socialist Workers Party. (50)

4C-53 "He Made Us All Feel Alive: Reactions to Malcolm's
       Death." Militant, 1 Mar 1965, p. 4.

       Reactions to the assassination from a number of
       people, including Martin Luther King and James Farmer.
       (1000)

4C-54 "Malcolm's Death Spotlights Gap Between Negro and
       White." National Guardian, 6 Mar 1965, p. 1.

       Criticism of the white press for its sensational
       coverage of Malcolm during his life. (500)

4C-55 "Young Socialists Send Message." Militant, 1 Mar
       1965, p. 4.

       Text of condolences from the Young Socialist
       Alliance. (100)

4C-56 "Militant Sends Condolences." Militant, 1 Mar 1965,
       p. 4.

       Text of condolences. (50)

4C-57   "Supporter of Malcolm X Faces Probe, Frame Up."
         Militant, 8 Mar 1965, p. 1.

         Story on Reuben Frances, an associate of Malcolm's,
who was arrested for shooting Talmadge Hayer at the
assassination scene. (400)

4C-58   "He Would Not Bow His Head to Any Tyrant."   Militant,
         8 Mar 1965, p. 1.
         .
         Story on Malcolm's funeral.   Lists some of the
prominent people who attended. (1000)

4C-59   "Interview with James Shabazz."   Militant, 8 Mar 1965,
         p. 3a.

         An interview with Malcolm's chief assistant.
Shabazz blames the assassination on the power
structure.   Also states that they intend to redouble
their efforts to build the OAAU. (1500)

4C-60   "Rowan's Smear of Malcolm X."   Militant, 8 Mar 1965,
         p. 1.

         Editorial criticizing Carl Rowan for his attack on
Malcolm.   Views Rowan's comments as a reflection of
Malcolm's popularity at home and abroad. (400)

4C-61   "Tribute Paid to Malcolm X."   Militant, 8 Mar 1965, p.
         8.

         Story on a memorial program held in Detroit. (250)

4C-62   "Speakers Pay Tribute to Malcolm X."   Militant, 15 Mar
         1965, p. 1.

         Story on a memorial program held in New York.
Includes lengthy quotes from speakers. (3000)

4C-63   "Text of Speech by James Shabazz."   Militant, 15 Mar
         1965, p. 3.

Speech by Shabazz at a memorial for Malcolm. (1000)

4C-64   "Bayard Rustin and Malcolm X." Militant, 15 Mar 1965,
        p. 4.

        Editorial criticizing Rustin for saying that Mal-
        colm was evolving towards a philosophy of nonviolence.
        (200)

4C-65   "Malcolm X: The Man and His Ideas." Militant, 22 Mar
        1965, p. 4, and 29 Mar 1965, p. 4.

        Same as citation #2-4.

4C-66   "British Guiana Youth Salute Malcolm X as a Heroic
        Fighter." Militant, 22 Mar 1965, p. 6.

        Text of a statement from the Progressive Youth
        Organization of British Guiana. (150)

4C-67   "Interview with Sister of Malcolm X." Challenge, 23
        Mar 1965, p. 1.

        An interview with Ella Collins. She blames the
        U.S. power structure for planning Malcolm's death and
        Elijah Muhammad for carrying it out. (200)

4C-68   "Fourth International Sees Death of Malcolm X as Blow
        to Oppressed Everywhere." Militant, 29 Mar 1965,
        p. 5.

        Text of statement by the Trotskyite Fourth Inter-
        national. (500)

4C-69   "African Reactions to Malcolm X's Death." Militant,
        29 Mar 1965, p. 6.

        Reactions from a number of African newspapers.
        (300)

4C-70   "200 Demonstrate in London over Murder of Malcolm X."
        Militant, 29 Mar 1965, p. 6.

        Story on a demonstration led by the Council of
African Organizations. (200)

4C-71   "Services in Indonesia for Malcolm X." Militant, 29
        Mar 1965, p. 6.

        Story of memorial services held in mosques, at the
request of the Minister of Religion. (200)

4C-72   "All Africa Was for Malcolm X." Militant, 5 Apr 1965,
        p. 4.

        Excerpt from a report of a tour by representatives
of SNCC. Includes comments on the reaction to Malcolm
in Ghana, Kenya, and Egypt. (500)

4C-73   "Chicago Memorial Meeting Aids Family of Malcolm X."
        Militant, 19 Apr 1965, p. 2.

        Story of a memorial held in Chicago. (300)

4C-74   "A Left-Wing Smear of Malcolm X." Militant, 24 May
        1965, p. 3, and 31 May 1965, p. 3.

        Article by Robert Vernon criticizing an article by
Bayard Rustin and Tom Kahn (citation #3-120). (5000)

4C-75   "OAAU Rally Marks Malcolm X Memorial Day." Militant,
        31 May 1965, p. 5.

        Story of a rally addressed by Ella Collins. (200)

4C-76   "Malcolm X's Murder and the New York Police."
        Militant, 12 July 1965, p. 1.

        Article by George Breitman on unanswered questions
about police involvement in the assassination. (1000)

4C-77 "More Questions on Malcolm X's Murder." Militant, 9
       Aug 1965, p. 2.

       Article by George Breitman. Questions the ability
       of the Nation of Islam to plan and carry out the
       assassination. (1500)

4C-78 "Jurors Are Selected in Malcolm X Case." Militant, 24
       Ja 1966, p. 2.

       List of names and occupations of the jurors. (300)

4C-79 "District Attorney Presents Case in Malcolm X Trial."
       Militant, 31 Ja 1966, p. 1.

       Update on trial. Discussion of the testimony of
       Carey Thomas, a bodyguard of Malcolm's. (2000)

4C-80 "Malcolm X Murder Trial." Militant, 7 Feb 1966, p. 2.

       Reviews testimony of George Whitney, an associate
       of Malcolm's. (2000)

4C-81 "Little Light Shed by Malcolm X Murder Trial."
       Militant, 14 Feb 1966, p. 2.

       Discussion of discrepancies in the testimony.
       (3000)

4C-82 "Malcolm X Murder Trial." Militant, 21 Feb 1966, p.
       2.

       Discussion of police testimony. (3000)

4C-83 "Confession Rocks Malcolm X Murder Trial." Militant,
       7 Mar 1966, p. 1.

       On Hayer's confession. (1000)

4C-84 "Malcolm X Murder Trial." Militant, 14 Mar 1966, p.
       3.

A summary of all of the testimony. (3000)

4C-85   "Who Killed Malcolm X?" <u>Militant</u>, 21 Mar 1966, p. 1.

Report on court verdict. Points out inconsistencies.

4C-86   "Three Get Life Terms in Malcolm X Case." <u>Militant</u>,
         25 Apr 1966, p. 3.

Report on the sentencing. (200)

4C-87   "Malcolm, King, Hampton: Victims of FBI Death Plot."
         <u>Militant</u>, 5 Apr 1974, p. 24.

Story on a call by Rev. Jesse Jackson to open an
investigation into the assassinations of Malcolm,
King, and Fred Hampton. Jackson points out that
recently released FBI documents point to a government
conspiracy. (500)

4C-88   "Ten Years Later: Who Killed Malcolm X?" <u>Militant</u>, 21
         Feb 1975, p. 24.

Article raising unanswered questions about the
assassination, including the role of the FBI and the
New York police. (2000)

4C-89   "Malcolm X and the FBI Cointelpro Operation."
         <u>Militant</u>, 18 Apr 1975, p. 14.

Discussion of the FBI's counterintelligence.
Quotes from FBI memos on the FBI's attempts to
destabilize the relations between the OAAU and the
Socialist Workers Party. (200)

4C-90   "Did the FBI Neutralize Malcolm X?" <u>Militant</u>, 18 Feb
         1977, p. 13.

An interview with Baxter Smith. He discusses FBI
involvement in the assassination. (1500)

4C-91 "The FBI and Malcolm X." <u>Militant</u>, 25 Mar 1977, p.
       16.

       Discussion on the FBI files compiled on Malcolm.
       (2500)

4D-1   "Malcolm States, Negro 'Tricked.'"   Daily Star
       (Beirut), 1 May 1964, p. 1.

       Report of speech by Malcolm in which he discusses
       the Afro-American perception of Africa. (250)

4D-2   "Help Negroes--Call to Africans."   Daily Express
       (Nigeria), 11 May 1964, p. 6.

       Report on a speech by Malcolm in Ibadan. He calls
       for building communication between Africans and Afro-
       Americans. (250)

4D-3   "Malcolm X."   Daily Graphic (Ghana), 12 May 1964, p.
       3.

       Note on Malcolm's arrival in Ghana and his plans to
       address the Ghana Press Club. (30)

4D-4   "X Is Here."   Ghanian Times, 12 May 1964, p. 12.

       Note on Malcolm's arrival in Ghana. (20)

4D-5   "Help U.S. Negroes: Malcolm X."   Daily Graphic
       (Ghana), 13 May 1964, p. 20.

       Malcolm's address to the Ghana Press Club. He
       states the need to internationalize the Afro-American
       struggle and praises Kwame Nkrumah. (300)

4D-6   "Civil Rights Issue in U.S. Is Mislabeled."   Ghanian
       Times, 13 May 1964, p. 3.

At a press conference, Malcolm calls for
internationalizing the Afro-American struggle and for
unity between Africans and Afro-Americans. Article
includes an announcement of a speech by Malcolm
sponsored by the Marxist Forum. (400)

4D-7   "Negroes Need Your Help, Says Mr. X." Daily Graphic
        (Ghana), 15 May 1964, p. 7.

        Malcolm's speech at the University of Ghana. He
        appeals for assistance from Africans to help the Afro-
        American people and compares the U.S. to South Africa
        in terms of its racial policies. Also praises
        Nkrumah, Ben Bella, and Nasser for their opposition to
        neo-colonialism, racism, and imperialism. (400)

4D-8   "African States Must Force U.S. for Racial Equality."
        Ghanian Times, 15 May 1964, p. 3.

        Speech in which Malcolm calls upon Africans for
        assistance to the Afro-American struggle. (400)

4D-9   "Malcolm Asibe." Ghanian Times, 16 May 1964, p. 5.

        Column in which the author gives Malcolm the Twi
        name of Asibe to replace X. He praises Malcolm for
        his mission to acquaint Africans with the struggle of
        Afro-Americans. (600)

4D-10   "Review of the Week." Ghanian Times, 16 May 1964, p.
        7.

        Note on Malcolm's appearance in Ghana. (150)

4D-11   "Malcolm X Addresses MP's." Ghanian Times, 17 May
        1964, p. 7.

        Note on a speech by Malcolm. (50)

4D-12   "Malcolm X and the Martyrdom of Rev. Clay Hewitt."
        Ghanian Times, 18 May 1964, p. 2.

Column in which the author criticizes Malcolm for his anti-white attitudes. He cites economic and class basis for racism, factors which he claims Malcolm ignores. (1000)

4D-13 "Malcolm X Really Back Home." Ghanian Times, 18 May 1964, p. 5.

Note on an exchange between Malcolm and several Ghanian students. (50)

4D-14 "X Speaks at Nkrumah Institute." Ghanian Times, 18 May 1964, p. 7.

Note that Malcolm spoke at the Kwame Nkrumah Ideological Institute. (75)

4D-15 "U.S. Negroes." Daily Graphic (Ghana), 21 May 1964, p. 3.

Note on Malcolm's welcoming a statement from Mao Ze Dong on the Afro-American struggle. (50)

4D-16 "Malcolm X." Daily Graphic (Ghana), 23 May 1964, p. 3.

Note on Malcolm's return to the U.S. (25)

4D-17 "Violence Will Grow in U.S.: Malcolm X." Egyptian Gazette, 27 July 1964, p. 2.

Report of speech by Malcolm in which he predicts more racial violence unless the U.S. government changes its racial policies. (300)

4D-18 "Malcolm X on Islam, U.S., Africa." Egyptian Gazette, 17 Aug 1964, p. 5.

Excerpts from an interview with Malcolm. (400)

4D-19 "Malcolm X Hails OAU." Egyptian Gazette, 23 Aug 1964,
       p. 2.

       Note on Malcolm's greeting to the Organization of
       African Unity. (150)

4D-20 "Malcolm X Visits U.K. 'Color Conscious' City." Daily
       Star (Beirut), 14-15 Feb 1965, p. 8.

       Report on Malcolm's visit to England. (100)

4D-21 "Malcolm X's Home Bombed." Daily Star (Beirut), 16
       Feb 1965, p. 8.

       Story on the firebombing of the home of Malcolm X.
       (100)

4D-22 "Malcolm X Shot Dead." Egyptian Gazette, 22 Feb 1965,
       p. 1.

       Report on the assassination. (250)

4D-23 "Malcolm's Death: Negroes Charged." Daily Express
       (Nigeria), 23 Feb 1965, p. 1.

       Report on the assassination. (300)

4D-24 "Malcolm Is Killed." Daily Graphic (Ghana), 23 Feb
       1965, p. 1.

       Article on the assassination. Statement from the
       All-Africa Trade Union Federation condemning U.S.
       imperialism for the assassination. (600)

4D-25 "Fight for Equality Rages On." Daily Graphic (Ghana),
       23 Feb 1965, p. 5.

       Editorial comment that Malcolm's death was a great
       blow to the Afro-American movement. (100)

4D-26   "Man Held in Malcolm X Killing." Daily Star (Beirut),
        23 Feb 1965, p. 1.

        Report on the arrest of the first of the suspected
        assassins. (200)

4D-27   "Malcolm X Knew Enemies Were Attempting to Kill
        Him." Daily Star (Beirut), 23 Feb 1965, p. 6.

        Story on Malcolm's suspicions that he was the
        target of an assassination attempt. (400)

4D-28   "Malcolm X Shot Dead." Daily Times (Nigeria), 23 Feb
        1965, p. 1.

        Article on the assassination. Quote from James
        Baldwin that there are "sinister implications" to the
        assassination. (300)

4D-29   "Malcolm X." Daily Times (Nigeria), 23 Feb 1965, p.
        5.

        Editorial recognizing Malcolm's less than universal
        appeal but still calls him a martyr. (500)

4D-30   "We Are Innocent: Muhammad." Egyptian Gazette, 23 Feb
        1965, p. 1.

        Report on Elijah Muhammad's disavowal of having any
        connection to the assassination. (200)

4D-31   "Police Blame Black Muslims for Killing." Egyptian
        Gazette, 23 Feb 1965, p. 1.

        Report on police speculation that the Nation of
        Islam was responsible for the assassination. (150)

4D-32   "Malcolm Murdered." Ghanian Times, 23 Feb 1965, p. 1.

        Article on the assassination, giving reactions from
        several civil rights leaders. (250)

4D-33 "Malcolm Will Live On." Ghanian Times, 23 Feb 1965,
       p. 6.

       Editorial praising Malcolm for his contribution to
       the Afro-American movement. Calls him a martyr. (500)

4D-34 "Shocking; Will They Mourn Him." Ghanian Times, 23
       Feb 1965, p. 7.

       Two letters to the editor expressing grief at
       Malcolm's death. (75)

4D-35 "Malcolm X Is Killed in Harlem Ballroom." Standard
       (Tanzania), 23 Feb 1965, p. 1.

       Report on the assassination. Incudes long quotes
       from statements issued by the ANC of South Africa and
       the South West African Peoples Organization (SWAPO).
       (500)

4D-36 "Malcolm X." Standard (Tanzania), 23 Feb 1965, p. 2.

       Editorial noting Malcolm's favorable impression in
       much of Africa. (300)

4D-37 "Malcolm: Muslim Mosque Blasted." Daily Express
       (Nigeria), 24 Feb 1965, p. 1.

       Note on the burning of the Nation of Islam's
       mosque. (100)

4D-38 "Suspicious Fire Damages 'Black Muslim' Mosque."
       Daily Star (Beirut), 24 Feb 1965, p. 8.

       Note on the burning of the Nation of Islam's
       mosque. (200)

4D-39 "Malcolm: Fire Guts Mosque." Daily Times (Nigeria),
       24 Feb 1965, p. 1.

       Note on the burning of the Nation of Islam's
       mosque. (150)

4D-40 "Black Muslim HQ Bombed, Gutted." Egyptian Gazette,
       24 Feb 1965, p. 1.

       Note on the bombing of the Nation of Islam's
       mosque. (150)

4D-41 "Malcolm X." Egyptian Gazette, 24 Feb 1965, p. 1.

       Editorial mourning the death of Malcolm. (400)

4D-42 "Malcolm X: A Tragic Loss." Ghanian Times, 24 Feb
       1965, p. 6.

       Article by Julian Mayfield. He calls Malcolm's
       death a setback for the Afro-American movement. Notes
       how Malcolm's views on capitalism and socialism
       changed. (1000)

4D-43 "Malcolm X's Body Laid in State." Ghanian Times, 24
       Feb 1965, p. 12.

       Note on the funeral arrangements and a memorial
       service held in Ghana. (200)

4D-44 "To the Memory of Malcolm X." Ghanian Times, 24 Feb
       1965, p. 6.

       Poem in honor of Malcolm X by MacNeil Stewart.

4D-45 "Mourners File Past Body of Malcolm X." Daily Express
       (Nigeria), 25 Feb 1965, p. 3.

       Note on Malcolm's funeral and the death threats
       against Cassius Clay. (200)

4D-46 "Nkrumah Sorry." Daily Express (Nigeria), 26 Feb
       1965, p. 3.

       Note on a message by Kwame Nkrumah to Malcolm's
       family. (40)

4D-47 "Kwame Sends His Sympathy." Daily Graphic (Ghana), 25
       Feb 1965, p. 1.

       Note on a message of condolence from Nkrumah and a
       memorial service held by the Association of Ghanian
       Writers and Journalists. (100)

4D-48 "Thousands in U.S. Mourn Malcolm X." Daily Graphic
       (Ghana), 25 Feb 1965, p. 2.

       Report on the memorial service in the U.S. (250)

4D-49 "Black Muslim Leader Threatened." Daily Star
       (Beirut), 25 Feb 1965, p. 1.

       Note on death threats against Elijah Muhammad.
       (150)

4D-50 "Malcolm X Stood for Racial Equality, Says Kwame."
       Ghanian Times, 25 Feb 1965, p. 1.

       Note on Nkrumah's message of condolence. (75)

4D-51 "This Is Political Murder, J. Farmer." Ghanian Times,
       25 Feb 1965, p. 1.

       Note on CORE Director James Farmer's reaction to
       the assassination. Also notes response of a Ghanian
       students organization, and various national liberation
       movements based in Ghana, all condemning U.S.
       imperialism. (300)

4D-52 "Grieving Still for Malcolm." Standard (Tanzania), 25
       Feb 1965, p. 5.

       Note on condolence messages by the PAC of South
       Africa and the NLM of Comoro. (200)

4D-53 "Police See Malcolm X Case Solved Shortly." Daily
       Star (Beirut), 26 Feb 1965, p. 8.

       Report on a police statement that a solution to the
       assassination is at hand. (200)

4D-54 "Malcolm: U.S. Accused." Daily Times (Nigeria), 26
       Feb 1965, p. 9.

       Report on a statement by the Council of African
       Organizations, a coalition of African student
       organizations in Europe, condemning U.S. imperialism
       for the assassination. (100)

4D-55 "Man Behind Killing of Malcolm X Known." Egyptian
       Gazette, 26 Feb 1965, p. 1.

       Report that the police know the identify of the men
       who killed Malcolm. (200)

4D-56 "Malcolm's Assassination Will Not End the Struggle."
       Ghanian Times, 26 Feb 1965, p. 1.

       Report on a statement by Julian Mayfield at a
       memorial service for Malcolm in Ghana. (400)

4D-57 "Afros to Hold Rally in Harlem." Ghanian Times, 26
       Feb 1965, p. 4.

       Note of a mass rally to be held by supporters of
       Malcolm in Harlem. (150)

4D-58 "Violent End." Daily Express (Nigeria), 27 Feb 1965,
       p. 4.

       Editorial expressing sympathy for Malcolm due to
       his violent death but notes no sympathy for his
       political outlook. (100)

4D-59 "Muslims Take U.S. to Task." Ghanian Times, 27 Feb
       1965, p. 4.

       Statement from the World Muslim Conference demand-
       ing a thorough investigation of the assassination.
       (100)

4D-60 "Second Man Charged in Malcolm X Slaying." Daily Star
       (Beirut), 27 Feb 1965, p. 8.

Note on the arrest of a second suspect. (75)

4D-61 "Tragic End of Malcolm X." Ghanian Times, 27 Feb
       1965, p. 7.

       Photo-essay on the assassination. Captions note
       that Malcolm stood for racial equality. (100)

4D-62 "Review of the Week." Ghanian Times, 27 Feb 1965, p.
       5.

       Note that most Afro-Americans reject the idea that
       Malcolm was killed by the Nation of Islam. (200)

4D-63 "Malcolm X Peacefully Laid to Rest." Daily Star
       (Beirut), 28 Feb-1 Mar 1965, p. 1.

       Article on the funeral of Malcolm. (200)

4D-64 "Police Want Third Man for Malcolm X Assassination."
       Egyptian Gazette, 1 Mar 1965, p. 1.

       Report on police attempts to locate a third suspect
       in the assassination. (150)

4D-65 "Elijah 'Not Afraid of Threats'." Egyptian Gazette, 2
       Mar 1965, p. 1.

       Report of Muhammad's statement on death threats.
       (150)

4D-66 "Malcolm X Aides Held." Daily Star (Beirut), 3 Mar
       1965, p. 8.

       Note that several of Malcolm's assistants were
       being held in the aftermath of the assassination.
       (100)

4D-67 "Third Man Held in Malcolm X Killing." Daily Star
       (Beirut), 5 Mar 1965, p. 8.

Note on the arrest of a third suspect in the
assassination. (75)

4D-68 "Third Man Held for Malcolm X Killing." Egyptian
       Gazette, 5 Mar 1965, p. 1.

       Note on the arrest of a third suspect in the
       assassination. (100)

5-1   2-17-53: Note that Malcolm was put on the Security
        Index Card kept by the FBI. The reason was that he
        had told someone that he was a communist. (1 page)

5-2   5-4-53: Description of Malcolm's criminal background.
        Makes note of a letter written by Malcolm, while in
        prison, in which he states he has always been a
        communist. Describes Malcolm's current membership
        in the "Militant Cult of Islam" (Nation of Islam),
        documenting his membership through Malcolm's
        correspondence with his brother. Several letters
        of the correspondence are included in the files.
        (10 pages)

5-3   6-8-53: Copy of a form for placing people on Security
        Index Cards. Malcolm is included because of his
        membership in the Nation of Islam. (2 pages)

5-4   3-16-54: Report that Malcolm is traveling as a Muslim
        minister. Gives location and dates of his visits
        to various Mosques. (14 pages)

5-5   4-12-54: Notes change of address on Malcolm's Security
        Index Card from Michigan to Philadelphia. (1 page)

5-6   4-30-54: Report that Malcolm had become the minister
        of the Philadelphia mosque. (1 page)

5-7   5-11-54: Report on Malcolm's parole status. (1 page)

5-8   8-23-54: Report that Malcolm has moved to New York to
        become minister of the New York mosque. (1 page)

5-9   8-31-54: Copy of Malcolm's Security Index Card. (1
        page)

5-10   9-7-54: Report that Malcolm had been preaching in the

Nation of Islam's mosques in New York and Boston. Also reviews the beliefs of the Nation of Islam. (4 pages)

5-11   9-22-54: Report on Malcolm's new address in Queens, New York. (2 pages)

5-12   11-19-54: Copy of a new Security Index Card for Malcolm. Surveys the beliefs of the Nation of Islam and summarizes the content of some of Malcolm's speeches. (10 pages)

5-13   11-30-54: Memorandum of Malcolm's background. (1 page)

5-14   1-28-55: Report on Malcolm's speeches in the New York mosque. Includes of summary of an interview with Malcolm by FBI agents. (15 pages)

5-15   5-23-55: Report describing Malcolm as a "paranoid schizophrenic"; details his education and work background. Provides detailed summaries of speeches given by Malcolm in New York, Detroit, Philadelphia, Chicago, and Springfield, MA, all delivered in mosques of the Nation of Islam. (30 pages)

5-16   5-25-55: Report on Malcolm's Selective Service record. Detailed summaries of several speeches given by Malcolm. Includes appendix, added in 1965, on the OAAU and the Muslim Mosque Inc. (9 pages)

5-17   1-31-56: Detailed reports on Malcolm's speeches in Nation of Islam mosques in New York, Philadelphia, Cincinnati, Hartford, CT, and Detroit. Includes long quoted sequences from the speeches. (116 pages)

5-18   4-30-58: Summary of Malcolm's activities in 30 cities. Most summaries give details of Malcolm's speech (all typical Nation of Islam eschatology), some reports merely note his presence in meetings. (136 pages)

5-19   7-2-58: Report noting that the FBI will consider Malcolm a "key figure" in light of his travels for the Nation of Islam. (1 page)

5-20   9-12-58: Report on Malcolm's presence in Atlanta. (1 page)

5-21   11-19-58: Report on Malcolm's importance in the Nation
       of Islam. Details his travels to 13 cities. (26
       pages)

5-22   11-26-58: Note on a threatening letter received by
       Malcolm. (1 page)

5-23   5-19-59: Summary of Malcolm's activities in 20 cities.
       Includes an appendix on the organization of the
       Nation of Islam. (53 pages)

5-24   7-17-59: Report asking for an investigation into
       whether Malcolm has a passport. (1 page)

5-25   7-21-59: Partial transcript of a documentary by Mike
       Wallace on the Nation of Islam entitled "The Hate
       that Produced the Hate." (30 pages)

5-26   7-13-59: Report that Malcolm was in Egypt and met with
       Gamel Nasser. (1 page)

5-27   5-17-62: Summary report on Malcolm. Details public
       activities, travels, and relationships with left-
       wing organizations. (35 pages)

5-28   2-12-62: Report on an appearance by Malcolm at
       Wesleyan University. Includes a summary of
       Malcolm's activities in 16 cities and contacts with
       several left-wing organizations. (30 pages)

5-29   7-21-59: Report that Malcolm was in the Middle East.
       (5 pages)

5-30   11-17-59: Report on Malcolm's activities in 7 cities,
       his trip to the Middle East, and more transcripts
       from the "Hate that Produced the Hate." (20 pages)

5-31   3-16-60: Transcript of a radio debate between Malcolm
       and Rev. William Jones on the topic of Black
       Supremacy, moderated by William Kunstler. (7 pages)

5-32   5-17-60: Report on Malcolm's activities in 7 cities,
       including appearances on radio programs in New
       York. (56 pages)

5-33   11-17-60: Report on Malcolm's activities in 15 cities.
       Notes political ambitions of Malcolm to run for
       Congress, and Malcolm's meeting with Fidel Castro
       during the latter's visit to Harlem. (30 pages)

5-34   5-17-60: Report on Malcolm's activities in 10 cities,
        contacts with the NAACP, the Ku Klux Klan, and
        several left-wing organizations. (26 pages)

5-35   4-6-61: Report on an appearance by Malcolm at Harvard
        University. (3 pages)

5-36   8-22-61: City-by-city summary of Malcolm's administra-
        tive activities within the Nation of Islam. (58
        pages)

5-37   5-19-61: Report on a visit to North Carolina by
        Malcolm. (3 pages)

5-38   11-16-62: Updated personal information on Malcolm,
        including a summary of activities. (26 pages)

5-39   2-4-63: Report on a local Washington, D.C. television
        appearance by Malcolm. (6 pages)

5-40   2-20-63: Note on Malcolm's travels. (3 pages)

5-41   3-13-63: Note on a speech by Malcolm in Charlotte, NC.
        (4 pages)

5-42   3-28-63: Report on a television appearance by Malcolm
        in New York. (1 page)

5-43   3-25-63: Report on a Nation of Islam rally in New
        York. (2 pages)

5-44   4-4-63: Copy of a statement by Malcolm at an NAACP-
        sponsored debate. (4 pages)

5-45   4-11-63: Report on an appearance by Malcolm in
        Buffalo. (2 pages)

5-46   5-14-63: Report on Malcolm's travel to Washington,
        D.C. Includes notes on the media coverage he
        received. (7 pages)

5-47   5-15-63: Reports on private meetings, public appear-
        ances, and public statements by Malcolm. (30 pages)

5-48   5-17-63: Report on a meeting between Malcolm and U.S.
        Representative Green. (3 pages)

5-49   3-31-64: Report that Malcolm had broken with the
        Nation of Islam to form the Muslim Mosque, Inc. (5
        pages)

5-50   5-27-64: Report on a press release by Malcolm about
        the Muslim Mosque, Inc. (2 pages)

5-51   5-19-64: Report on a warrant issued for Malcolm to
        appear in court for a speeding ticket. Notes that
        he was traveling in Africa and the Middle East at
        the time. (1 page)

5-52   4-24-64: Report on Malcolm's travel arrangements in
        Africa. (6 pages)

5-53   3-31-64: Note that Malcolm has broken with the Nation
        of Islam and set up the Muslim Mosque Inc. (3
        pages)

5-54   5-21-64: Note on Malcolm's arrival time in New York
        from Paris. (1 page)

5-55   5-27-64: Report on the Muslim Mosque Inc. Information
        compiled from legal papers of incorporation and a
        press release. (3 pages)

5-56   5-20-64: Updated background report on Malcolm. (2
        pages)

5-57   5-19-64: Report that a warrant had been issued for
        Malcolm's arrest on a traffic violation. (1 page)

5-58   5-19-64: Addition of the name "El-Hajj El Shabazz" to
        Malcolm's personnel file. (1 page)

5-59   4-30-64: Report on a debate in Chicago between Malcolm
        and Louis Lomax. (2 pages)

5-60   4-30-64: Report on an eviction notice filed by the
        Nation of Islam against Malcolm. (1 page)

5-61   4-24-64: Report on Malcolm's travel plans while in
        Africa. (3 pages)

5-62   4-14-64: Report that Malcolm has departed New York for
        Egypt. (1 page)

5-63   4-7-64: Report on the formation of a rifle club in
        Cleveland. Notes that Malcolm had publicly called
        for· such a formation. (3 pages)

5-64   4-7-64: Report on a CORE-sponsored rally held in
        Cleveland with Malcolm as a speaker. Quotes
        Malcolm's comments on forming rifle clubs. (3
        pages)

5-65   4-14-64: Report on a speech by Malcolm at a rally
        sponsored by the Group on Advanced Leadership
        (GOAL) in Detroit. Quotes from Malcolm's "Ballots
        or Bullets" speech. (3 pages)

5-66   4-20-64: Another report on the eviction efforts. (2
        pages)

5-67   4-17-64: Report on a request by the State Department
        for information on several of Malcolm's associates
        who may be traveling abroad. Includes speculation
        on Malcolm's ability to draw members away from the
        Nation of Islam. (6 pages)

5-68   4-27-64: Report on a school boycott in Chicago. (2
        pages)

5-69   4-20-64: Memo to regional offices ordering them to
        check on local mosques of Nation of Islam and
        identify those members thought close to Malcolm. (5
        pages)

5-70   3-3-64: Report on a speech by Malcolm at Harvard. (7
        pages)

5-71   3-31-64: Note on an appearance by Malcolm on "Kup's
        Show" in Chicago. (2 pages)

5-72   3-31-64: Report on the media coverage of Malcolm in
        Chicago. (5 pages)

5-73   3-27-64: Note of a request by the District Attorney of
        Louisiana for information on Malcolm. (3 pages)

5-74   3-9-64: Report on a communication between Malcolm and
        a Muslim in Miami. Malcolm relates his views on
        integration. (2 pages)

5-75   3-13-64: Report on a press conference by Malcolm
        announcing the formation of the Muslim Mosque
        Inc. Includes text of release (citation #1-5(2))
        and a summary of Malcolm's answers to questions.
        (10 pages)

5-76   3-11-64: Report on a TV appearance by Malcolm. States
        he still believes in the Nation of Islam's
        philosophy. (2 pages)

5-77   3-13-64: Note on a request for J. Edgar Hoover to
        comment on Malcolm's statements about forming rifle
        clubs. Includes text of request (a letter). (3
        pages)

5-78   2-20-64: Report on Malcolm's visit to Florida as a
        guest of Cassius Clay. (1 page)

5-79   2-12-64: Report on an FBI interview with Malcolm
        (citation #1-40). Includes the text of the Playboy
        interview (citation #1-52). (15 pages)

5-80   2-10-64: Report on the widening rift between Malcolm
        and Elijah Muhammad. (1 page)

5-81   5-??-64: Report on the formation of the Muslim Mosque
        Inc. (3 pages)

5-82   6-9-64: Report on Malcolm's appearance on a radio
        show. Summarizes his comments on his visit to
        Africa. (3 pages)

5-83   6-16-64: Report of a meeting between Malcolm and
        several members of the Communist Party, discussing
        Malcolm's idea to approach the UN on the Afro-
        American question. (6 pages)

5-84   6-24-64: Note on threats against Malcolm's life. (2
        pages)

5-85   6-18-64: Copy of file on Malcolm covering his activi-
        ties, public and private meetings, from 1963 to
        date. Includes information on his relations with
        civil rights and left-wing organizations. (66
        pages)

5-86   7-2-64: Report on an appearance by Malcolm in Omaha.
        Quotes Malcolm's changed position on separation.

Includes summarized question and answer period. (11 pages)

5-87   6-26-64: Report on a scheduled radio appearance in Chicago. (2 pages)

5-88   7-7-64: Report on Malcolm's visit to Africa. (10 pages)

5-89   7-31-64: Report on Malcolm's scheduled return from Africa. Notes the extensive coverage he has received from the Militant newspaper. (8 pages)

5-90   8-10-64: Report on a meeting between Malcolm and the Islamic Federation of the U.S., in Egypt. (3 pages)

5-91   8-26-64: Copy of an interview with Malcolm by A. B. Spellman (citation #1-2(1)), originally published in French. (14 pages)

5-92   9-10-64: Copy of a Saturday Evening Post excerpt from Malcolm's autobiography. Includes a copy of Malcolm's memo to the OAU (citation #1-5(7)). (17 pages)

5-93   10-9-64: Report that Malcolm has become an orthodox Muslim. (1 page)

5-94   10-1-64: Report from the State Department that Malcolm called on the U.S. Embassy in Kuwait to obtain a copy of a lost health certificate. (1 page)

5-95   10-5-64: Copy of a New York Times article stating that Malcolm has rejected all racist doctrines. (3 pages)

5-96   10-2-64: Report that a Maoist newspaper in Switzerland is giving Malcolm a lot of press. (2 pages)

5-97   10-16-64: Exchange of letters between the FBI and a New York lawyer concerning Malcolm's whereabouts. (3 pages)

5-98   1-20-65: Lengthy file on Malcolm. Gives his background, break with the Nation of Islam, his UN plans, connections and meetings with left-wing groups, foreign travel, and includes lengthy excerpts from a number of speeches. (132 pages)

5-99 2-2-65: Short report on an OAAU rally. Summary of
      Malcolm's "Ballots or Bullets" speech. (9 pages)

5-100 2-3-65: Report on Malcolm's travel arrangements to
       Alabama and London. (1 page)

5-101 2-25-65: Report of a bomb threat at the funeral home
       where Malcolm's body is lying in state. (1 page)

5-102 2-26-65: Copy of the UPI report on the assassination.
       (3 pages)

5-103 2-25-65: Request to interview a reporter with knowl-
       edge of the Revolutionary Action Movement (RAM) to
       determine if they were involved in Malcolm's assas-
       sination or the burning of the Nation of Islam's
       mosque in New York. (6 pages)

5-104 2-22-65: Detailed report of the assassination. (12
       pages)

5-105 2-23-65: Report that two FBI informants were in the
       ballroom at the time of the assassination. (2
       pages)

5-106 2-19-65: Translated copy of an article on Malcolm that
       appeared in a Chinese magazine. (1 page)

5-107 2-24-65: Report on a bomb threat to the funeral home
       where Malcolm's services will be held. (4 pages)

5-108 2-24-65: Report of an FBI informant who was at the
       assassination scene. (10 pages)

5-109 2-17-65: Report of a meeting between Malcolm and
       Wallace Muhammad. (3 pages)

5-110 2-23-65: Report on activity in the Washington, D.C.
       mosque surrounding Malcolm's death. (2 pages)

5-111 2-24-65: Report of intent to investigate any inter-
       national implications of Malcolm's assassination.
       (1 page)

5-112 2-22-65: Copy of Malcolm's autopsy report. (2 pages)

5-113 2-23-65: Another FBI informant who was present at the
       scene gives his report on the assassination. (2
       pages)

5-130   11-15-63: File on Malcolm, including speaking
        engagements and meetings. (30 pages)

5-131   2-23-67: Report on a memorial march in New York for
        Malcolm. (2 pages)

5-132   4-14-66: Note on the sentencing of Hayer, Butler, and
        Johnson. (6 pages)

5-133   9-8-65: Report on the assassination and a list of
        Malcolm's activities in 1964 and 1965. (58 pages)

5-134   3-26-68: Note on plans to produce a movie about
        Malcolm's life. (1 page)

5-135   4-25-69: Copies of several book reviews of published
        speeches of Malcolm's. (8 pages)

5-136   4-19-72: Reports from various FBI offices about local
        memorials for Malcolm. (30 pages)

VI BOOK REVIEWS

Autobiography of Malcolm X. New York: Grove
Press, 1965.

6-1   Anthony Adair. Contemporary Review. :49, July 1966.

6-2   Robert Bone. New York Times. 11 Sept 1966, p. 3.

6-3   Emile Capouya. Saturday Review. 20 Nov 1965, p. 42.

6-4   R. L. Caserio. Cambridge Quarterly, 4:84, Wint 1969.

6-5   Bell Gale Chevigny. Village Voice. 3 Mar 1966, p. 18.

6-6   John Henrik Clarke. Freedomways. 6:48, Wint 1966.

6-7   Economist. 18 June 1966, p. 1314.

6-8   Eliot Fremont-Smith. New York Times. 5 Nov 1965, p.
        39.

6-9   Ruth Glass. Listener. 22 Sept 1966, p. 428.

6-10   Geoffrey Godsell. Christian Science Monitor. 11 Nov
        1965, p. 11.

6-11   Oscar Handlin. Atlantic. 216:150, Dec 1965.

6-12   Nat Hentoff. Commonweal. 28 Ja 1965, p. 511.

6-13   Len Holt. Liberator. 6:22, Feb 1966.

6-14   Thomas Kretz. Christian Century. 8 Dec 1965, p.
        1513.

6-15   Doris Lessing. New Statesman. 27 May 1966, p. 755.

6-16   Colin MacInnes. Spectator. 27 May 1966, p. 668.

6-17   A. Mayhew. Commonweal. 3 Dec 1965, p. 288.

6-18   Truman Nelson. Nation. 8 Nov 1966, p. 336.

6-19   Newsweek. 15 Nov 1965, p. 130.

6-20   Carter Partee. Community. 25:10, Feb 1966.

6-21   Bayard Rustin. Book Week. 14 Nov 1965, p. 1.

6-22   Raymond Schroth. America. 22 Apr 1967, p. 594.

6-23   Richard Small. Race. 8:190, Oct 1966.

6-24   I. F. Stone. New York Review of Books. 11 Nov 1965,
        p. 3.

6-25   Earl Thorpe. Social Education. 33:489, Apr 1969.

6-26   Times Literary Supplement. 9 June 1966, p. 507.

6-27   John Woodford. Negro Digest. 15:51, Dec 1965.

                By Any Means Necessary. New York: Pathfinder,
                1970.

6-28   Angela Blackwell. Black Scholar. 1:56, May 1970.

6-29   Lee Smith. International Socialist Review. 31:54,
        May 1970.

6-30   Times Literary Supplement. 28 May 1971, p. 605.

                End of White World Supremacy. New York: Merlin
                House, 1971.

6-31   Guardian Weekly. 18 Dec 1971, p. 19.

6-32   Julius Lester. New York Times Book Review, 16 May
        1971, p. 4.

                Malcolm X Speaks. New York: Merit, 1967.

6-33   W. E. Brockeriede. Quarterly Journal of Speech.
        52:411, Dec 1966.

6-34   Len Holt. Liberator. 5:22, Feb 1966.

6-35   David Llorens. Negro Digest. 15:89 May 1966.

6-36   Raymond Schroth. America. 116:594, 22 Apr 1967.

6-37   I. F. Stone. New York Review of Books. 11 Nov 1965,
       p. 4.

       Speeches of Malcolm X at Harvard. New York:
           Morrow, 1968.

6-38   P. Jefferson. Quarterly Journal of Speech. 54:314,
       Oct 1968.

6-39   New York Times Book Review. 13 Apr 1969, p. 24.

6-40   Time. 23 Feb 1970, p. 88.

       Baldwin, James. One Day When I Was Lost: A
           Screenplay Based on the "Autobiography of
           Malcolm X". New York: Dial, 1973.

6-41   Anthony Bailey. New Statesman. 3 Nov 1972, p. 643.

6-42   Bruce Cook. Commonweal. 12 Oct 1973, p. 46.

6-43   Times Literary Supplement. 17 Nov 1972, p. 1390.

       Breitman, George. Last Year of Malcolm X: The
           Evolution of a Revolutionary. New York:
           Merit, 1973.

6-44   George Novack. International Socialist Review.
       28:43, July-Aug 1967.

       Clarke, John. Malcolm X: The Man and His
           Times. New York: Macmillan, 1969.

6-45   Charles V. Hamilton. New York Times Book Review. 28
       Sept 1969, p. 3.

6-46   William Hamilton. Christian Century. 11 Feb 1970, p.
       177.

6-47   Time. 23 Feb 1970, p. 88.

6-48   Virginia Quarterly Review. 46:1XX, Spr 1970.

Essien-Udom, E. U. Black Nationalism.
Chicago: University of Chicago Press, 1962.

6-49   A. D. Grimshaw. Annals of the American Academy of
       Political and Social Sciences. 344:188, Nov 1962.

6-50   Kyle Haselden. Christian Century. 22 Aug 1962, p.
       1010.

6-51   Nat Hentoff. Commonweal. 27 July 1962, p. 428.

6-52   G. E. Lang. American Journal of Sociology. 68:376,
       Nov 1962.

6-53   August Meier. American Historical Review. 68:260,
       Oct 1962.

6-54   Lillian Smith. Saturday Review. 45:33, 23 June 1962.

6-55   Times Literary Supplement. 21 Sept 1962, p. 727.

Goldman, Peter. Death and Life of Malcolm X.
New York: Harper, 1973.

6-56   David Brudnoy. National Review. 6 July 1973, p. 747.

6-57   Andrew Buni. America. 24 Mar 1973, p. 267.

6-58   R. E. Burns. Critic. 31:71 Mar-Apr 1973.

6-59   Bruce Cook. Commonweal. 12 Oct 1973, p. 46.

6-60   Orde Coombs. New York Times Book Review. 28 Ja 1973,
       p. 40.

6-61   Arthur Cooper. Newsweek. 8 Ja 1973, p. 61.

6-62   R. H. Evans. Christian Century. 28 Mar 1973, p. 372.

6-63   Loyle Hairston. Freedomways. 13:160, No. 2, 1973.

6-64   Stephen McKenna. Best Sellers. 32:558, 15 Mar 1973.

Jamal Hakim. From the Dead Level: Malcolm X
and Me. New York: Random House, 1972.

6-65 C. C. Ware. Saturday Review. 55:52, 1 July 1972.

6-66 Times Literary Supplement. 12 Nov 1971, p. 1407.

Lincoln, C. Eric. Black Muslims in America.
Boston: Beacon, 1961.

6-67 M. E. Burgess. Social Forces. 40:196, Dec 1961.

6-68 Kenneth Clark. Saturday Review. 44:23, 13 May 1961.

6-69 James Ivy. Crisis. 68:377, June-July 1961.

6-70 R. M. James. American Journal of Sociology. 67:213,
Sept 1961.

6-71 Peter Kihss. New York Times Book Review. 23 Apr
1961, p. 6.

6-72 Herb Nipson. Chicago Tribune. 14 May 1961, p. 2.

6-73 J. M. Yinger. Annals of the American Academy of
Political and Social Sciences. 338:199, Nov 1961.

Lomax, Louis. When the Word Is Given.
Cleveland: World Publishing, 1963.

6-74 R. S. Bird. Book Week. 29 Dec 1963, p. 9.

6-75 John LaFarge. America. 9 Nov 1963, p. 584.

6-76 John LaFarge. Saturday Review. 46:42, 14 Dec 1963.

6-77 Willie Morris. Nation. 13 Ja 1964, p. 56.

6-78 Newsweek. 4 Nov 1963, p. 107.

Maglangbayou, Shawna. Garvey, Lumumba, and
Malcolm: National-Separatists. Chicacgo:
Third World Press, 1972.

6-79 Black World. 21:51, Oct 1972.

Paris, Peter. <u>Black Leaders in Confict: Joseph H. Jackson, Martin Luther King, Jr., Malcolm X, and Adam Clayton Powell, Jr.</u> New York: Pilgrim Press, 1978.

6-80   G. S. Wilmore. <u>Christian Century</u>. 11 Oct 1978, p. 963.

Randall, Dudley, and Burroughs, Margaret. <u>For Malcolm: Poems on the Life and Death of Malcolm X</u>. Detroit: Broadside Press, 1969.

6-81   Conrad Rivers. <u>Negro Digest</u>. 16:68, June 1967.

Wolfenstein, Eugene. <u>The Victims of Democracy: Malcolm X and the Black Revolution</u>. Berkeley: University of California Press, 1981.

6-82   Miriam Ershkovitz. <u>Annals of the American Academy of Political and Social Sciences</u>. 461:186, May 1982.

6-83   Joel Kovel. <u>Nation</u>. 23 May 1981, p. 644.

6-84   Howard Zinn. <u>American Historical Review</u>. 87:289, Feb 1982.

AUTHOR INDEX

Adair, Anthony 6-1
Adegbalola, Gaye Todd 3-1
Adoff, Arnold 2-37
Allen, Robert 3-2
Andrews, James 1-11
Bailey, A. Peter 3-3,3-4
Bailey, Anthony 6-41
Baldwin, James 2-1,3-5,3-6
Baraka, Amiri 3-7
Barbour, Floyd 1-26
Barnes, George 4B-155
Bates, Eveline 3-8
Benson, Thomas 3-9
Berthoff, Werner 3-10
Berton, Pierre 1-44
Bethune, Lebert 3-11
Bird, R. S. 6-74
Black, Pearl 3-12
Blackwell, Angela 6-28
Boggs, James 3-13,3-14
Bone, Robert 6-2
Booker, James 4B-181
Borders, James 3-15
Bosmagian, Haig 1-23
Boulware, Marcus 3-16
Bradly, David 3-17
Breitman, George 2-2,2-3,
    2-4,3-18,3-19,4C-10,
    4C-14,4C-18,4C-76,4C-77
Brockeriede, W. E. 6-33
Brudnoy, David 6-56
Bryce, Tony 4B-155
Bunche, Ralph 4B-88
Buni, Andrew 6-57
Burgess, M. E. 6-67
Burns, R. E. 6-58
Campbell, Finley 3-20
Capouya, Emile 6-3
Caserio, R. L. 6-4

Chevigny, Bell Gale 6-5
Clark, Kenneth 1-47,6-68
Clarke, John Henrik 2-5,
    3-22,3-23,6-6
Clasby, Nancy 3-24
Cleague, Albert 3-25,3-26,
    3-27,3-28
Cleaver, Eldridge 3-29,
    3-30,3-31
Coles, Robert 3-32
Cook, Bruce 6-42,6-59
Coombs, Orde 6-60
Cooper, Arthur 6-61
Crawford, Marc 3-33
Curtis, Richard 2-38
Davis, John 3-34
Davis, Lenwood 2-6
Davis, Ossie 3-35,3-36,
    3-37,3-38,4B-177
Deck, Alice 2-7
Demarest, David 3-40
Diamond, Stanley 3-39
Doudu, Cameron 3-41
DuBois, Shirley Graham 3-42
Dunayevskaya, Raya 4C-11
Eakin, Paul 3-43
Elmessiri, Adelwahab 3-44
Epps, Archie 1-7,2-8,3-45
Ershkovitz, Miriam 6-82
Essien-Udom, E. U. 2-9,3-46
Essien-Udom, Ruby 3-46
Evans, R. H. 6-62
Farmer, James 1-21,1-22,1-23
Farrakhan, Louis 4B-113,
    4B-118,4B-128,4B-138
Flick, Hank 3-47,3-48,3-49
Foner, Phillip 1-12,1-28
Freemont-Smith, Eliot 6-8
Gardner, Jigs 3-50

185

SUBJECT INDEX

189